the

baby owner's

games and activities book

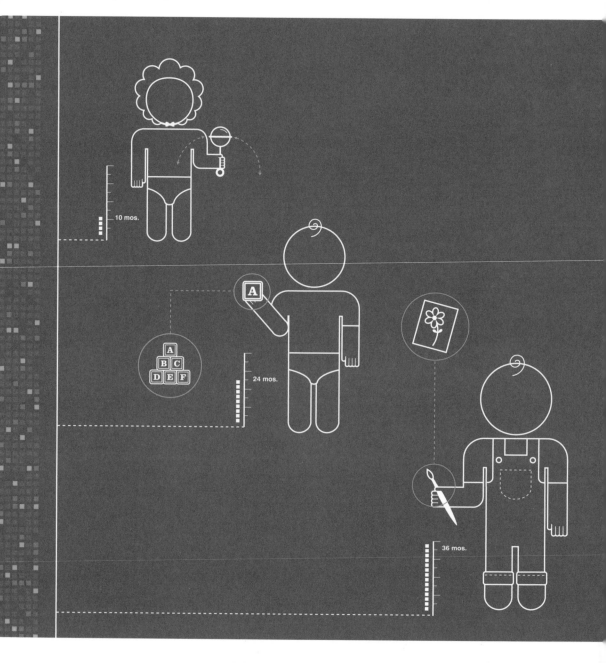

the
baby owner's
games and activities book

BY LYNN ROSEN AND JOE BORGENICHT

ILLUSTRATED BY

PAUL KEPPLE AND JUDE BUFFUM

QUIRK BOOKS
PHILADELPHIA

Library of Congress Cataloging in Publication Number: 2006900714

ISBN-10: 1-59474-060-7
ISBN-13: 978-1-59474-060-2

Printed in Singapore

Typeset in Swiss and Digital

Designed by Paul Kepple and Jude Buffum @ Headcase Design
www.headcasedesign.com

Distributed in North America by Chronicle Books
85 Second Street
San Francisco, CA 94105

10 9 8 7 6 5 4 3 2 1

Quirk Books
215 Church Street
Philadelphia, PA 19106
www.quirkbooks.com

Contents

Congratulations on the arrival of your new baby!

The baby is surprisingly similar to other appliances you may already own. Like a personal computer, for instance, the baby will require a source of power to execute her many complicated tasks and functions. Like a videocassette recorder, the baby's head will require frequent cleanings for optimum performance. And like an automobile, the baby may expel unpleasant odors into the atmosphere.

By now you have probably familiarized yourself with your model's many functions. This process of learning how your model operates will be ongoing, as your model will continue to develop and display new capacities throughout its lifetime.

This manual has been prepared to help you facilitate the expansion and improvement of your model's abilities. *The Baby Owner's Games and Activities Book* provides 75 age-appropriate activities for user and model to execute together, all of which contribute to your model's growth. Activities are divided into three sections, one for each of your model's first three years.

Consider the activities in *The Baby Owner's Games and Activities Book* part of the required maintenance and upkeep for which you are responsible. Regular usage and manipulation will help your unit's parts to function properly.

By using the activities contained herein, the model user will gain a thorough and advanced understanding of all the many interlinked functions available. These activities will ensure proper development, and will also provide many stimulating hours together for model and owner.

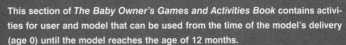

Part 1

This section of *The Baby Owner's Games and Activities Book* contains activities for user and model that can be used from the time of the model's delivery (age 0) until the model reaches the age of 12 months.

During this first year of growth, your model will begin to gain some of the following abilities:

- Visual sensors will see greater distances; auditory sensors will detect more sounds.
- Grasping mechanisms will be able to pick up objects and manipulate small objects.
- Model will learn to hold up head, sit up, and crawl, and may enter early walking mode.
- Solid food consumption will commence.

Each activity in this section addresses one or more of these developmental stages.

Users may select any age-appropriate activity desired from this section of the manual; it is not necessary to proceed in the order they appear. The manufacturer does recommend that users try all of the activities, however, since each contributes in a different way to the model's development. Try each activity, select favorites, and repeat them as often as desired.

Once you have had the model 12 months or more, users are encouraged to move on to the next section of the book. However, feel free to return to these activities as long as they interest your model.

BABY DANCE STEPS

FUNCTION

It is never too early to expose your model's auditory sensors to music. Add movement to music, and the model will be soothed and comforted.

REQUIRED ACCESSORIES

Source of music and various albums (Fig. A).

OPERATION

■ Activate music while the model is being held by the user (Fig. B). Gently move to the rhythm of the music. The user may stand still and rock side to side, or step, sway, and move around the room. The user may choose to hold the model cradled in her arms, position the model upright with model's head on user's shoulder, or hold the model out with head supported by user's hands or arms (Fig. C). Continue swaying and/or stepping patterns to give the model a sense of a continuous loop.

VARIATIONS

Rock the model to music while the model is placed in a cradle. Accompany other types of movement, such as in a stroller or a car, with music.

CAUTION

The model's muscles, particularly in the neck, are not ready to sustain rapid movement. Always hold the model carefully and keep movements slow and gentle. Always support the model's head and neck.

(Fig. A)

(Fig. B)

(Fig. C)

Rythmic movement and musical sounds
will soothe and stimulate the model.

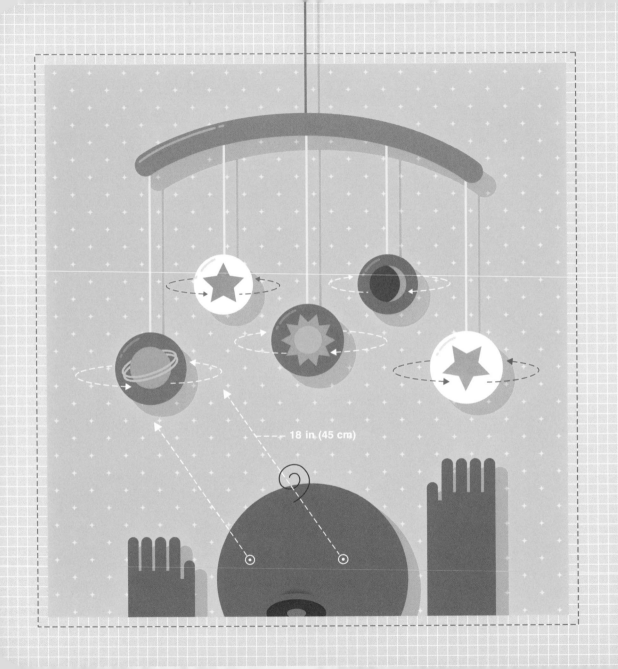

18 in. (45 cm)

MOBILE MOTION

FUNCTION

Engaging visual sensors. Your unit's visual sensors currently have a limited distance range, and hence are attracted to bold black and white high-contrast patterns. In addition, while the model has limited control of his hand extensions, this will not prevent him from beta-testing these appendages.

REQUIRED ACCESSORIES

A mobile with dangling black and white graphic designs, or individual toys with similar markings.

OPERATION

■ Attach mobile over the model's crib or place model on a blanket on the floor and hold mobile/toys over model. Be sure that mobile/toys hang within approximately 18 inches (45 cm) of the model's visual sensors, as the model's distance vision programming is not yet activated. Touch or shake the patterned objects so they move gently in front of the model. The model will watch closely as the designs rotate. Model may also reach out and swipe at the objects.

VARIATIONS

Place stationary black and white pictures at eye level near the model's crib for frequent viewing.

CAUTION

Do not leave toys with strings within reach when the model is unsupervised.

VOICE PATTERN RECOGNITION

FUNCTION

Engaging audio sensors. Having heard its female user's voice during nine months of factory assembly, your model will now orient its head toward this sound. New units also tend to prefer soft, gentle, high-pitched (i.e., female) vocal patterns. This activity stimulates the model's vocal recognition skills.

REQUIRED ACCESSORIES

Female user voice.

OPERATION

■ Enter a room where the unit has been placed. Before the unit's visual sensors detect your presence, call out to unit. Call out the model's name, or utter other phrases (e.g., "Mommy's here!" or "Sweetie Pie!") in a sing-song voice. Observe as the unit turns toward your voice.

■ This activity can continue after the unit discovers your location. The user can duck out of visible range and call to the unit, and then suddenly pop back into view. The user should not remain out of view for more than several seconds at a time.

■ *NOTE:* Your unit's visual sensors will remain closed for most of the first few days after delivery. This is an excellent opportunity to beta-test the vocal recognition program. Female user should remain in close proximity to unit, ideally cradling unit in her arms, while talking, cooing, and singing to unit.

CAUTION — If the unit is consistently unresponsive to sound, call your service provider immediately.

YOGA BABY

FUNCTION

Increasing flexibility. Ideal for newer models, this activity will stretch limbs accustomed to more crowded factory conditions. As models age, these exercises will help with body extension awareness, use, and balance.

REQUIRED ACCESSORIES

A soft mat, towel, or blanket.

OPERATION

■ Place newer models (0–6 months) face up on blanket or mat. Gently pull one leg to a straight, fully extended position. Repeat with second leg and then with each arm. Do leg and arm lifts with the extended limbs. Place the model with extended legs and arms straight at sides, and gently roll model from side to side. Hold the model upright and suspend her in a standing position with feet on the ground. Then, with the model again on her back, take feet and gently bend knees up toward her face. While in this position, again gently roll from side to side.

■ Turn older models (7–12 months) on their stomachs, with heads turned to the side. Lift up feet one at a time, bending the model's knee gently back. Then lift the model by the hips, raising her bottom into the air, so that she is in an inverted V, with hands and feet touching the ground. As the model ages, she will be able to support this position by herself.

VARIATIONS

Older models can continue with gentle yoga poses. Consult outside sources for further instruction.

CAUTION Make all movements gentle and slow; desist if the model displays any discomfort.

FOLLOW MY FINGER

FUNCTION

Engaging and enhancing visual sensors. After just one month of use, your model's visual sensors will detect objects up to 12 inches (30 cm) away.

REQUIRED ACCESSORIES

A human hand with five fingers.

OPERATION

▪ Place the model face up on a rug or blanket. Hold your hand approximately 12 inches (30 cm) above the model's visual sensors. Extend one finger. Observe to see if your model notices. Move your finger to one side. Repeat until the model recognizes and tracks the finger.

▪ Once your model is trained to follow a single finger, you can introduce additional fingers and vary the motion. Wave all five fingers together. Open and close the fingers in a fist. Rotate your wrist in a circle. Move your hand away from the model's face to gauge the limits of its vision. As your model ages, it will be able to watch your hand from greater distances.

VARIATION

You can alter this activity using finger puppets found on pages 134–135.

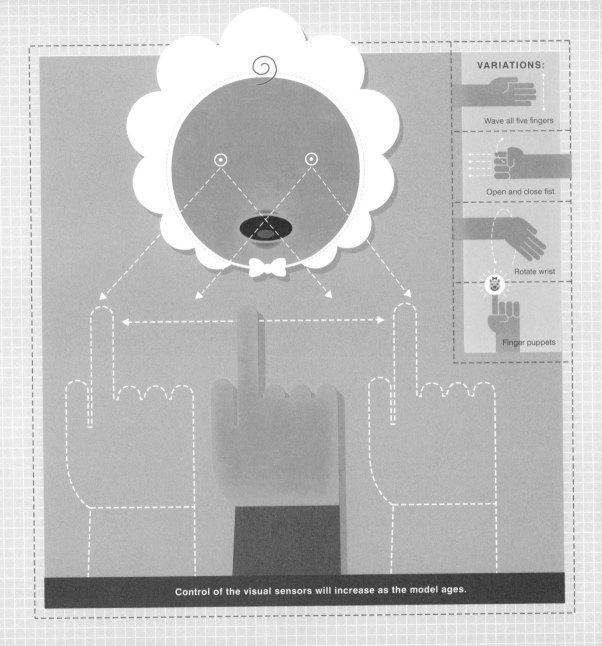

VARIATIONS:

Wave all five fingers

Open and close fist

Rotate wrist

Finger puppets

Control of the visual sensors will increase as the model ages.

FLYING BABY

FUNCTION

This activity relaxes the model before placing him in sleep mode, or soothes a model that is emitting mood error messages. It also strengthens the muscles connecting the model's head (which is disproportionately large at this age) to its chassis.

REQUIRED ACCESSORIES

None.

OPERATION

■ The user should hold the model in what is commonly referred to as the "football hold," with the user's arm extended and the model placed on his stomach on the user's arm, with head on or over user's hand. Once the model is in position, the user rocks model side to side and front to back, and walks around the room, gently swinging the model in this mock airplane ride. The user may choose to accompany these movements with "vroom" sounds.

VARIATIONS

Hold the model upright from behind, supporting him under his arms. Swing him back and forth like a pendulum for a different flying sensation. Or cradle the model in both arms for a makeshift swing.

CAUTION Do not drop the model. Support the neck if the model cannot do so himself.

TUMMY TIME

FUNCTION

Your unit contains a complex system of movement enablers, commonly referred to as *muscles*. This factory-installed system is sealed within the unit to prevent tampering. However, external manipulation by the user is encouraged to ensure this system continues to function and expand at the proper rate. This activity will help to develop the movement enablers that lift the unit's head.

REQUIRED ACCESSORIES

A comfortable and flat floor surface.

OPERATION

■ Announce to the unit in a cheerful voice that "It's tummy time!" Place the unit bottom side up on chosen flat surface. Watch while the unit responds and adjusts to this new position. Encourage the unit to lift his head. Cheer for the unit when this feat is accomplished.

■ The more the user pursues this activity, and the older the unit becomes, the more the unit will be able to achieve, lifting the head higher and pushing up on the arms. This muscle development will later assist the unit in the sitting and standing functions.

VARIATIONS

Place the unit on a variety of surfaces. Use mats, towels, and rugs with different textures. Use blankets with bright colors and vivid designs. Talk, sing, or play soothing music during the activity.

CAUTION

Some units may experience discomfort during this activity. Discontinue activity if the unit is extremely unhappy. Finally, remember that the unit must never be placed face down during sleep mode.

BABY TALK

FUNCTION

Accelerating the use of language. At 2 months, your model will begin to emit cooing sounds, which are the first steps toward language implementation. By acknowledging and repeating these sounds, the user can encourage the development of the unit's speaking function.

REQUIRED ACCESSORIES

Human vocal chords.

OPERATION

■ Listen to the sounds your unit makes. Engage your unit in "conversation" by repeating these sounds back to her. Gradually add simple new sounds to the conversation, or make a song of the sounds and sing them back to the model.

VARIATION

It is also important to speak to the model in adult language and syntax, so that she becomes familiar with the sounds of advanced language usage.

REFLECTION DETECTION

FUNCTION

Your unit has many moving parts and extensions, but is largely unaware of the full extent of her surface area. This activity provides a useful run-down of functional parts.

REQUIRED ACCESSORIES

Mirror.

OPERATION

- ■ Place or hold the unit in front of a mirror. Help and guide her as she discovers that this is her reflection.

- ■ Start slowly, allowing the model to gaze at her reflection for some minutes as she begins to realize that she is viewing her own image. Then begin to talk to her about what she is seeing. The user can playfully ask, "Who's that?" and can begin to point out body parts: nose, mouth, head, ears, and so on.

VARIATIONS

The user may also appear in the mirror alongside the unit. This will help the unit recognize that what she is seeing is a reflection. Put your face next to hers and say, "Look, there's Mommy/Daddy." Pop in and out of view for a game of reflective peek-a-boo. The user can make faces at his or her reflection to encourage the unit to do the same.

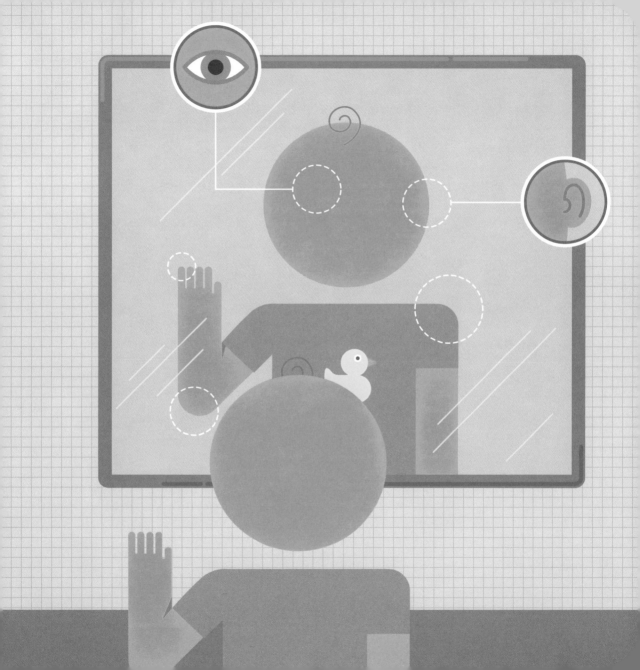

CLAP YOUR HANDS / SHAKE YOUR RATTLE

FUNCTION

Accelerating motor functions. At age 3–6 months, your model will begin to recognize that his hand extensions can move, reach, and grasp. He will spend much time studying the functionality of these attachments. In these activities, the user will demonstrate and teach the model both the clapping function of hands and the reaching and grasping maneuver.

REQUIRED ACCESSORIES

CLAP YOUR HANDS: Model and user sets of hands.

SHAKE YOUR RATTLE: Model and user sets of hands, plus small rattles, toys, and stuffed animals.

OPERATION

■ **CLAP YOUR HANDS:** The user should begin activity with a demonstration. Hold hands in front of the model, and make the clapping motion. Describe what you are doing. Then, if the model does not imitate the motion, gently take the model's hands and demonstrate how to clap. Spend some time clapping together. Clap in rhythmic patterns, clap alternately noisily and softly, or clap to accompanying music.

■ **SHAKE YOUR RATTLE:** Either following Version 1.0 above or in a separate session at a different time, the user can initiate the reaching and grasping part of the tutorial. Place the small rattle, stuffed animal, or other toy in front of the model, just out of his reach. Comment on the toy's proximity and encourage the model to reach out and pick up the toy. You may begin with the toy easily in reach and then slowly move it further away, not so far as to tease or frustrate the model, but far enough to encourage him to stretch out and reach for the toy.

FEATHER TICKLES

FUNCTION

Understanding her body and its features. Every day, your model will learn more and more about the extent of her body parts, their connectivity, and how she can power them up. Use this playful activity to help her gain familiarity with her body.

REQUIRED ACCESSORIES

Soft clean feather, preferably of the germ-free synthetic variety.

OPERATION

■ Wave feather in front of the model's eyes. Then begin to touch feather to the model's body. Tickle the model's tummy. Tickle her feet and toes. Work your way methodically through all body parts, naming them as you go. The model will enjoy close proximity to the user as well as being tickled by the feather, and will simultaneously be labeling and storing names of body parts in her memory cache.

■ *NOTE:* This activity is most effective if the model is clothed only in a diaper for maximum skin-to-feather interaction.

VARIATIONS

As always, vocalizations during activities are left to user preference. Instead of naming body parts, you may wish to simply utter "kitchie kitchie" or any cheerful sound of your choice.

CAUTION Do not leave the model alone with the feather. It can be a choking hazard.

BICYCLE LEGS

FUNCTION

Developing the muscles that operate the unit's leg extensions.

REQUIRED ACCESSORIES

Two human hands belonging to user; two leg extensions attached to unit.

OPERATION

■ Place the model on its back on any flat, comfortable surface. Attach your hands to the unit's ankles. Slowly begin to move the unit's ankles in forward circles, one after the other, as if the unit were peddling a bicycle. After some time, reverse the motion, as if the unit were peddling backward.

■ *NOTE:* This is a useful activity to undertake during diaper installation.

VARIATIONS

Accompany these movements with sound, either parental singing or music generated by an electronic device.

CAUTION

Keep all movements slow and gentle. Inappropriate stretching of movement enablers (also referred to as *muscles*) can cause discomfort and may lead to malfunction.

DRUM TUMMY

FUNCTION

Another benefit of exposing your model to music is to encourage the recognition of rhythmic patterns. By treating your model as a type of instrument and tapping patterns on its outer surface, you will enhance its ability to recognize musical patterns.

REQUIRED ACCESSORIES

None.

OPERATION

■ Use your model as if he were an instrument. Place your model on his back, sing or play a pre-recorded song, and gently tap a rhythm on the model's tummy. Or softly rub the model's cheek to the beat. Hold the model on your lap and clap his hands and stamp his feet along with the rhythm of the music.

VARIATIONS

Teach the model to be his own musical instrument by clapping his hands, slapping his knees, or stamping his feet. More advanced older models can progress to Let's Have a Parade, page 72.

 CAUTION Always be gentle. At 3–12 months, your model will not be compatible with the music of Queensryche, Mötley Crüe, and other heavy metal bands.

OLFACTORY STIMULATION

FUNCTION

Your model comes equipped with a relatively sophisticated olfactory sensor. Keep this feature in working order by introducing your model to a variety of pleasant scents.

REQUIRED ACCESSORIES

Any scent-producing object in your environment.

OPERATION

■ Flowers are a convenient and compact source of scent. If the user and model pass a garden while walking, point out the flowers and hold a fragrant variety near the olfactory sensor. Pantomime the sniffing motion to show the model how to pick up the scent. Be alert for other pleasant odors throughout the day and give the model an opportunity to become aware of their scents as well. Present the model with a variety of things to sniff, such as freshly cut peaches or berries, fresh baked goods, herbs, shampoo and soap, crayons, and more.

MAKING FACES

FUNCTION

Your model can already display a variety of facial expressions, including those communicating pleasure and discomfort. As her emotional range expands, train her to utilize new ways of signaling feelings by manipulating her facial muscles.

REQUIRED ACCESSORIES

User and model facial muscles.

OPERATION

■ Your model will receive maximum pleasure when the user manipulates his own facial array in amusing and entertaining ways. Make a variety of silly and funny faces for the model to observe. The user may accompany these faces with equally entertaining and/or silly sounds. The user may incorporate movements such as blinking eyes, sticking out tongue, etc. The user may augment this standard repertoire in any way desired.

■ The user should follow the entertaining part of the activity with some more instructional faces, accompanied by descriptive language. For example, the user should explain that he is happy and make happy faces. He should make faces that represent other emotions: sad, angry, tired, etc. In this way the model will absorb standard facial expressions and learn what they represent. Eventually, the model will be able to replicate these faces.

VARIATIONS

Props such as hats, masks, clown noses, Groucho glasses, and other disguises may be incorporated into the activity.

SING A SONG

FUNCTION

As mentioned elsewhere in this manual, your model has been programmed with a special vocal recognition program. By age 3 months, this program will most likely have absorbed a number of songs and rhymes. You can activate additional functions of the vocal recognition program by challenging pattern recognition—in other words, by presenting familiar tunes in unfamiliar ways.

REQUIRED ACCESSORIES

A passable singing voice, knowledge of basic nursery rhymes.

OPERATION

■ Choose one very familiar rhyme to begin, for example "Twinkle, Twinkle, Little Star" (see page 132). Sing this to the model in your usual manner. Then begin to introduce a number of variations. Sing the song quickly; sing it very slowly. Sing it in a high- and a low-pitched voice. Sing it in a jazzy, country, rock-and-roll or hip-hop style. Sing it any way you can imagine. Aside from entertaining the model, hearing a familiar tune sung in a different way will challenge his auditory processing skills.

VARIATIONS

Use other songs supplied in the appendix on page 119.

MINI MAYPOLE

FUNCTION

Your model's vision is now almost perfect, but he will still benefit from tracking objects as they move. He sees shapes and colors clearly and enjoys spotting them in his environment.

REQUIRED ACCESSORIES

Empty paper towel roll, colorful ribbons or steamers. Tape the ribbons or streamers to the end of the roll to make the mini maypole.

OPERATION

■ Hold the mini maypole where the model can see it. Begin to twirl it and wave it so that the attached ribbons spin all around. The model will extend grasping mechanisms and attempt to tug on the ribbons (make sure they are securely attached). Maintain twirling motion. The model's visual sensors will track and absorb this colorful display.

VARIATIONS

Activate multiple programs and add a muscle development aspect to the activity by holding the object just outside the model's range of vision, so he has to stretch his neck or turn his body to see the mini maypole. Older models may hold and shake the mini maypole themselves.

PLAYING WITH PEAS

FUNCTION

Your unit's grasping devices (also referred to as *hands*) will become increasingly sophisticated as the unit ages. After about 6 months, the unit will acquire the ability to grasp and pick up small items. You can accelerate the model's development by performing the following activity.

REQUIRED ACCESSORIES

Peas, fresh or frozen, cooked to soften and cooled to room temperature.

OPERATION

■ Place your unit in her eating station and buckle her in safely. Place peas on the tray in front of your model, either alone or mixed with other edibles. Encourage the model to attempt to pick up peas.

■ *NOTE:* You will want to carefully clean in and around the eating station after this activity, as these tiny green items can slip and squish into unexpected places.

VARIATIONS

Use other small consumable items instead of peas, such as baked beans, or small pieces of baked tofu. Just make sure all foods are very soft and easy to digest without chewing (e.g., no raisins or nuts).

CAUTION

As the model's ability to pick up small items increases, so does the risk of small inappropriate items finding their way into the model's mouth. Be vigilant and make sure that small loose items are not within the model's reach, as these constitute a serious choking hazard.

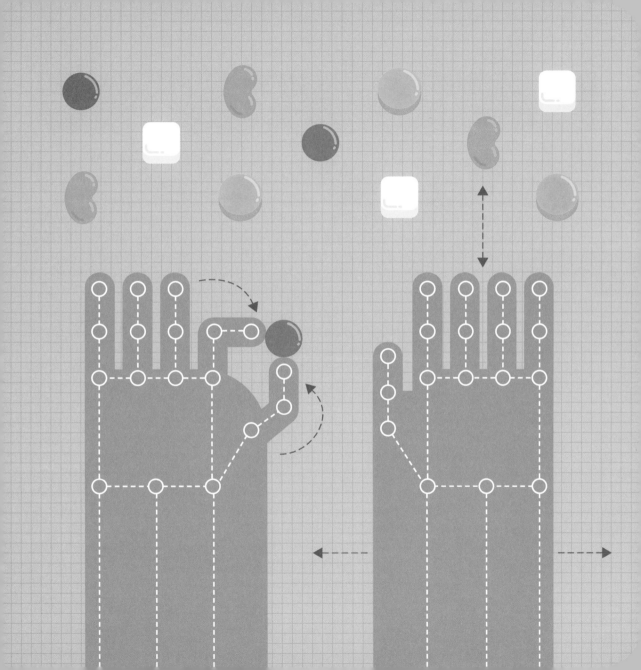

PEEK-A-BOO

FUNCTION

At this age, your model will begin to grasp the concept of object permanence (i.e., that user has not disappeared just because he is not currently visible). This allows for the introduction of basic-level Object Displacement, known in user-lingo as *peek-a-boo*.

REQUIRED ACCESSORIES

Only hands are necessary to cover or hide the user's face, however, other objects—scarves, books, stuffed animals—can also be used to obscure user visage.

OPERATION

■ The user should stand where he is visible to the model. The user should then cover his face, being sure the model notices this mock "disappearance." The user should then suddenly reveal himself while uttering the phrase "peek-a-boo!" Continue the game as long as it retains the model's interest (or as long as user can endure), introducing additional accessories, as described above, where appropriate or needed.

VARIATION

The user may introduce the game, before hiding his face, by asking model: "Where's Daddy?" or "Where is [name or label of user]?"

COUNTING FINGERS AND TOES

FUNCTION

Your model's symmetrical finger and toe extensions are conveniently positioned for early counting exercises. At 6–12 months, your model's numerical pattern recognition program is not fully operational. But the data collected in this activity will be stored in model's memory cache for future use when the program is functioning in full.

REQUIRED ACCESSORIES

Model's finger and toe extensions.

OPERATION

■ Hold up the model's hand or foot so the model can see it. Begin to count while grasping fingers and/or toes one at a time. Count repeatedly from one to ten, and then from ten back down to one.

■ Make other variations by showing the model how to clasp together thumb and several fingers, so that they are holding up only one, two, three, or four fingers.

■ *NOTE:* The user may wish to store this activity in her memory bank and reactivate it when the model is age 4 years or older for practice with addition, e.g., 5 + 5 = 10.

VARIATIONS

The traditional nursery rhyme "This Little Piggy Went to Market" (see page 131) is another finger or toe counting exercise that can be utilized during this activity. The model's fingers and toes are also suitable for pretend nibbling; the user can nibble and count.

ROLL PLAY

FUNCTION

Your model will be able to sit fully upright at about 6 months of age. With the model placed in this newly attainable upright position, the user and the model will be able to execute a new range of activities.

REQUIRED ACCESSORIES

Balls of different sizes and weights, such as plastic inflatables that will roll slowly, or smaller rubber balls that move more quickly.

OPERATION

■ Place the model on the floor in a seated position and sit facing the model, approximately 2–3 feet (60–90 cm) away. The user may wish to sit in the spread-eagle position, with legs extended to create a sort of playing field. This position will prevent the ball from rolling too far off course.

■ Roll ball toward the model. Ball will stop when it reaches the model's legs. Encourage the model to pick up ball. Then show the model, by guiding her arm movements, how to respond by rolling the ball back to the user.

■ This activity requires extensive repetition while the model learns to understand and then to repeat the movements required to roll the ball. As the model masters this skill set, the user may increase distance between the user and the model, and may also roll the ball at a faster pace.

VARIATIONS

Introduce a board or plank, and roll the ball down the length of it, lifting it at either end to create a slide. Or try rolling two balls at once.

CAUTION

At the younger end of this age range, your model will be able to remain in an upright seated position for as long as 30 minutes. This period will increase as the model ages.

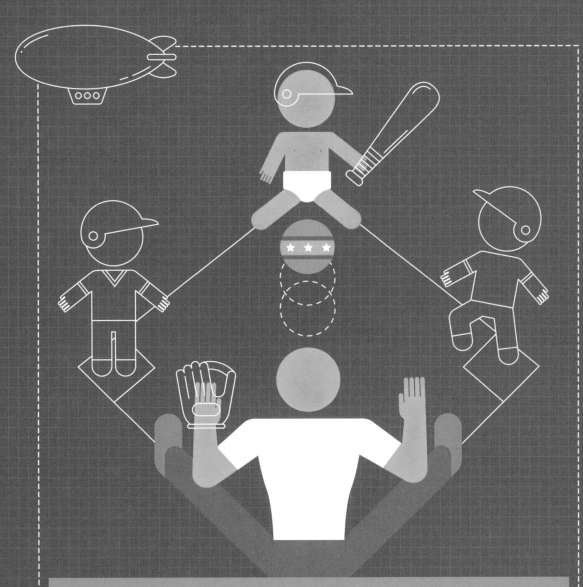

As the model masters this skill, increase your distance to keep the game challenging.

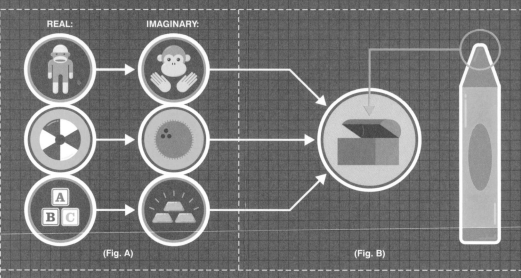

REAL: IMAGINARY:

(Fig. A)

(Fig. B)

(Fig. C)

Even the most ordinary household items will seem fresh and exciting to your unit.

TREASURE CHEST, VERSION 1.0

FUNCTION

The model is developing a sense of spatial relationships. This activity focuses on the concepts of "in" and "out."

REQUIRED ACCESSORIES

A sturdy and visually appealing container with a lid that opens and closes easily. The optimal selection is a canister that is 6 to 12 inches (15–30 cm) in height. This will be the treasure chest. Fill it with a selection of small (but not so small that they fit in model's mouth) toys, blocks, and other colorful, easy-to-grasp items (Fig. A and B).

OPERATION

■ Place the model in a seated position on the floor; place the treasure chest next to the model. Show the model how to open the container. Help her remove the items in the treasure chest one by one, taking time to play with each item as it is removed (Fig. C). Once the container is empty, help the model replace the contents, again one by one. Repeat this in and out process; allow the model to self-activate as much as possible.

VARIATION

The next time you run this activity, activate model's surprise reflex by filling the container with different contents.

KITCHEN BAND

FUNCTION

Your model has a preprogrammed interest in banging objects together to create sound. Stimulate this attraction to early forms of music by giving her access to noise-making objects.

REQUIRED ACCESSORIES

Pots, pans, or other kitchen containers (and their lids) to serve as drums; wooden spoons or plastic utensils (without sharp edges) for drumsticks.

OPERATION

■ Arrange pots and other items on the floor; place the model on floor in seated position next to them. Or keep all of these items in a low kitchen cabinet, and let the model explore and pull the items out herself. Encourage the model to bang and hit and otherwise generate any sounds she can, all of which will be pleasing to her ear.

■ *NOTE:* The user may find it convenient to activate Kitchen Band while the user is preparing food.

 CAUTION Never keep anything of danger (e.g., cleaning solutions, heavy pots) in a kitchen cabinet that is accessible to children. Always use child safety locks on cabinets where appropriate.

TUG-OF-WAR

FUNCTION

Test your model's developing and improving grasping abilities in this user-model interface experiment.

REQUIRED ACCESSORIES

Long scarf (or any dangling toy).

OPERATION

■ Place the model on back on blanket or carpet. Dangle scarf over the model's head/chest area, just within reach of his extended arms and hands. Encourage the model to reach for the object. Just as the model's hand nears the scarf, pull it playfully out of reach. Repeat this several times for the model's pleasure. Then allow the model to grasp the object, and gently pull on the other end, creating a casual tug-of-war. Alternate the waving and pulling away of object and the tugging handshake interface.

 CAUTION Although the model's arm extensions have been securely installed, you should avoid pulling hard on these extensions.

FUN IN A BOX

FUNCTION

Owners who have purchased numerous play-oriented baby accessories may have noted a common (and disappointing) phenomenon: The model is often more interested in the box itself than whatever came in it. This activity exploits the model's interest in boxes and turns that interest into an opportunity for creativity.

REQUIRED ACCESSORIES

Empty, clean cardboard box of size larger than the model.

OPERATION

■ Place box on floor; place the unit adjacent to box. No further intervention is necessary. Observe as the model interacts with box and crawls in, under, and around it.

VARIATIONS

Give the box an actual designation. Pretend it is a house or a playground toy. Decorate the box to make it resemble one of these objects, or attach two or more boxes together to create a tunnel in which the unit can practice entry and exit techniques.

CAUTION

Do not leave the unit unsupervised. The unit may become trapped in the box or attempt to climb on the unsupported structure.

The adult user can employ crayons to decorate the box. Very young children should not play unsupervised with crayons.

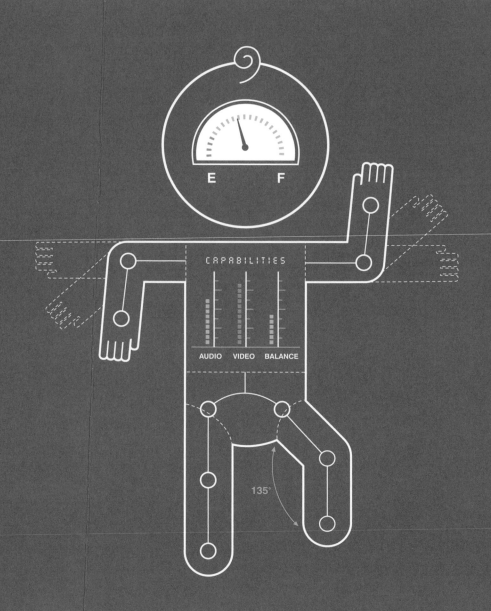

CAPABILITIES

E   F

AUDIO   VIDEO   BALANCE

135°

Part 2

13-24
MONTHS

This second section of *The Baby Owner's Games and Activities Book* contains activities for user and model that are appropriate from age 13 months (i.e., the beginning of the model's second year of life) until the model reaches the age of 24 months, or two years.

During this second year of growth, your model will begin to gain some of the following abilities:

- Increased mobility with propulsion apparatus, including walking, running, and jumping.

- Improved grasping ability and related motions, including throwing and drawing.
- Comprehension of concepts such as colors, temperature, and properties of water.
- Preliminary recognition of letter and number characters.
- Increased vocabulary of anywhere from 20 to 100 words.

Each activity in this section addresses one or more of these developmental stages.

Again, try them all, mix and match, repeat favorites, and come back to them as often as possible. Your model will benefit from repetition and from trying out new skills and abilities every day.

BALL IN A BUCKET

FUNCTION

Once your model can manage the standing function independently, she is ready for exercises of balance and dexterity.

REQUIRED ACCESSORIES

Lightweight balls that are easy for the model to grasp, a bucket or basket of some type.

OPERATION

■ Place the model in upright standing position in proximity to bucket or basket. Place ball in her hand. Using another ball, demonstrate to model how to toss ball into bucket.

■ A large supply of tossable items is recommended, as this will minimize the user's need to bend and fetch items that have missed the target.

VARIATION

Toss other small soft items such as stuffed animals or lightweight plastic toys.

PLAYING WITH GOO

FUNCTION

At this age, your model likely enjoys random pattern creation (e.g., scribbling).

REQUIRED ACCESSORIES

Homemade finger paint goo (made by mixing 2 parts cornstarch with 1 part water). Add food coloring until the desired hue is attained.

OPERATION

■ Place mix on clear, clean surface. Allow the model to engage in multiple processing techniques with this goo: squishing, smearing, squeezing, piling, spreading, swirling, etc. Additional functions may also emerge from the unit's growing memory cache. The goo will harden as it dries.

■ *NOTE:* The user will wish to have a designated location in the home for this and other mess-generating activities. If food coloring is used, it can be removed from hands with multiple washings.

CAUTION — **Mixture is nontoxic and not harmful if ingested. Nonetheless, since the model may enjoy placing things in his oral cavity, consumption of mixture should be strongly discouraged.**

COLOR RECOGNITION

FUNCTION

At this age, your model's color recognition and distinction program is almost fully functional. Running this program frequently will eliminate any remaining kinks.

REQUIRED ACCESSORIES

None. This activity can be performed in virtually any location with objects at hand.

OPERATION

■ Establish and announce the goal for the activity: "Let's look for things that are blue." Look around the room in which the user and model are currently stationed, then carry or walk with the model around the house. Seek objects that are blue. If the model does not see an object, user may narrow the search field, as in: "Do you see something blue on that shelf?" Once an object is located, discuss, touch, or hold the object, and then return to search/find mode. Once one color search has been completed, implement a new search for a different color.

VARIATIONS

This activity can be conducted in any interior or exterior locale, or even in a moving vehicle. It can also be used to distract the model during routine chores such as grocery shopping.

CARTON BLOCKS

FUNCTION

Your model likely enjoys stacking blocks, since she now has the dexterity to do so.

REQUIRED ACCESSORIES

Clean, empty, cardboard cartons leftover from orange juice, milk, etc.

OPERATION

Present your model with a pile of these homemade carton blocks. They are large enough that your model can easily grasp them. As with any activity, the user should first demonstrate how objects are to be used, so the model can encode and duplicate user movements. Encourage the model to stack carton blocks one on top of another, making as big a pile as she can. The user should emit laughing sounds when carton blocks fall and initiate an automatic repeat request.

VARIATIONS

Many objects can be successfully stacked, including blocks and stacking toys made specifically for this purpose.

 CAUTION Avoid containers made of glass or metal. These could injure the model.

ART CLASS

FUNCTION

Your unit will have enhanced grasping skills at this stage, as well as a sense of color and shape. This activity combines these skills and produces creative output.

REQUIRED ACCESSORIES

Large paper or drawing pad and fat crayons.

OPERATION

■ Place the unit in front of paper and crayons (Fig. A). Demonstrate how to pick up and hold a crayon, and show the model how the crayon makes marks on the paper. Emphasize that crayons must not be eaten (Fig. B). Show how different crayons make different colors, explaining as you go along. Encourage the unit to pick up and manipulate the crayons (Fig. C). Specify certain colors, as in: "Can you draw me a red picture?" to encourage the model to search for and locate a red crayon.

■ *NOTE:* This activity has the additional benefit of creating artworks suitable for framing.

VARIATION

If the unit tires of this activity, introduce a guessing game. The user may create simple drawings of easily recognizable objects for the unit to identify.

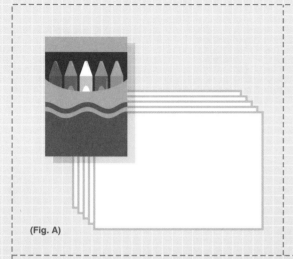

(Fig. A)

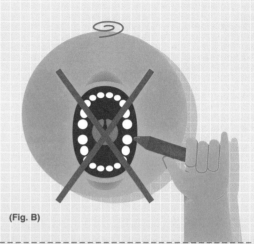

(Fig. B)

(Fig. C)

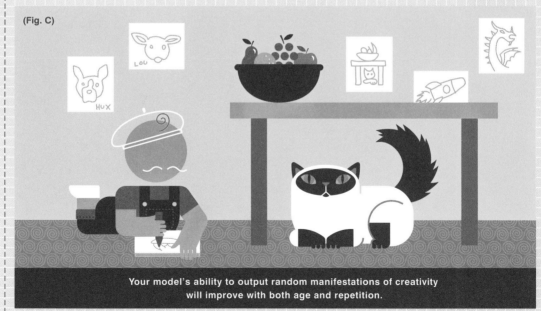

Your model's ability to output random manifestations of creativity
will improve with both age and repetition.

SNOW IN A BOX

FUNCTION

As your model's grasping skills become more sophisticated, challenge him with this slippery natural material.

REQUIRED ACCESSORIES

This is a seasonal activity and requires meteorological cooperation. When there is snow outside, collect some in a small plastic box and bring it inside.

OPERATION

■ Place the box of snow in front of the model. Allow the model to manipulate the snow, touching it and moving it around and learning its properties. Help him pack it into balls and other shapes. Try stacking these shapes together and building things. For added interest, tell him you will place the snow aside for use later, and return to discover to his surprise that it has melted into water.

VARIATIONS

Sand can also be used for a similar experience and is more suited for year-round usage.

CAUTION

Remember that your model will be sensitive to extreme hot and cold temperatures. As such, the model should only handle snow for short periods at a time.

BUCKET OF FUN

FUNCTION

Your model likely enjoys endless water play. Use this interest as an entry technique to other educational concepts.

REQUIRED ACCESSORIES

Bucket, water, and toys and other immersible small objects.

OPERATION

■ Fill a bucket with water and surround it with several toys or objects. Hold a single toy above the bucket. Ask the model if he thinks this object will sink or float, and demonstrate the difference by placing object on surface of water, and then holding it beneath the surface. Then ask the model to drop the object into the bucket. Together, model and user should monitor how object responds. One by one, drop other objects into bucket (user may wish to remove earlier objects to reduce crowding) to watch whether they float or sink. Encourage the model to guess prior to immersion which they will do.

VARIATIONS

The user should choose a variety of objects, heavy and light, porous and nonporous, perforated and solid. This activity can also take place in a sink, a bathtub, a swimming pool, or other water-filled container.

NAME GAME

FUNCTION

The letter recognition program self-activates at different ages in different models. However, it is never too early to begin to point out letters so that units can familiarize themselves with their shapes. It is sensible to begin practice for letter and word recognition by pointing out the letters that form the model's name, especially since there will likely be numerous gifts given to the unit with this series of letters visibly imprinted upon them.

REQUIRED ACCESSORIES

Anything with the model's name on it, such as personalized gifts, or any objects marked with the letters that make up the model's name, such as blocks, rubber floor tiles, plastic bathtub letters, or writing or drawing implements.

OPERATION

■ Show the model an example of his name spelled out. Say the name aloud, and explain, "This is your name." Do this repeatedly. Carry the model around his room, pointing out places where his name is written. Take out paper and write the model's name while the model watches; place a crayon in the model's hand and help him to form his name. Write the model's name on sticky notes and place them on the model's belongings.

CAUTION Take care not to overemphasize the naming of possessions, as this may lead to difficulty when model is required to activate shareware.

PAINT YOUR BELLY

FUNCTION

This activity adds play to the routine of bath time.

REQUIRED ACCESSORIES

Liquid baby bath soap, small container, food coloring, washcloth.

OPERATION

■ Before you begin, pour a small amount of liquid baby bath soap into a container; add a few drops of and mix. Fill the bathtub with several inches of warm water. Place the model on a bathmat adjacent to the tub. Use a wet washcloth to moisten the model's surface (do not oversaturate). Then apply colored soap to the model's surface.

■ Once the model is covered in color, user can paint shapes and letters on the model's belly and body parts. Continue activity as long as desired. Finish by placing the model in bathtub and washing off soap. Your unit is fully immersible.

CAUTION

Excessive application of food coloring may cause temporary discoloration of the model. Do not try the activity before an important photo opportunity. Also, never leave the model unattended in water, even for a few seconds.

ACCOMPANIMENTS:

castanets   egg shakers   flags

⚠ HAZARD:

Never leave model alone with scarves.

BABY DANCE PARTY

FUNCTION

At this point, your model is probably up and running—literally. With every passing day, the model discovers new ways to control her gross motor skills. Dancing to music is an excellent way to further this development.

REQUIRED ACCESSORIES

Music, a selection of sheer scarves.

OPERATION

■ Activate music in a location where there is space to run around. Begin to move to the music (e.g., dance), encouraging the model to do the same. Run, jump, hop, skip, or otherwise move around the room. The user should then bring out a scarf, and wave it around the model, toreador style. Hand the model a scarf of her own to wave around. Continue dancing and playing with scarves in creative ways. Wave them overhead. Drape one loosely over the model's head (make sure the scarf is sheer enough to see through).

VARIATIONS

Use other objects to accompany the dancing: castanets, egg shakers, flags, or paper towel rolls with streamers attached to the ends.

CAUTION Never use the scarf in a way that could choke the model. After you have finished playing, store the scarves in a safe location.

SHAVING CREAM ART

FUNCTION

This activity will advance your model's ability to recognize and reproduce the letters used to form words.

REQUIRED ACCESSORIES

Shaving cream and a designated mess-proof flat tabletop area. Food coloring optional.

OPERATION

■ Spray some shaving cream over the surface of a clean flat table surface. If desired, add a few drops of food coloring. Have model insert fingers and hands into this foamy matter. Encourage model to mix and play with it (and, if you wish, add a few more drops of food coloring). Draw a letter in the shaving cream and encourage the model to duplicate your actions. Repeat the same letter several times before beginning a new one.

VARIATIONS

Make some shapes in shaving cream on a piece of stiff construction paper. Allow to dry and hang for display. Also, numbers and shapes can be substituted for letters.

CAUTION Ingesting shaving cream will lead to model malfunction.

SING IN THE BLANK

FUNCTION

Your model is comforted by the soothing and repetitive sounds of her favorite nursery rhymes. Use her familiarity with these songs to activate her language acquisition and utilization functions.

REQUIRED ACCESSORIES

User vocal chords.

OPERATION

■ Sing the model's favorite songs. Pause before singing the last word of each line. Indicate to the model that she should fill in the missing word. For example, sing, "Twinkle, twinkle, little _____, how I wonder what you _____." The model will quickly realize the objective, and will insert the missing word when needed. An enjoyable sing-along will ensue. Do this with any of the model's favorite songs, or use the lyrics provided on pages 120–132.

VARIATIONS

Once the model is familiar with this activity, leave blanks at unexpected times in the song, not just at the end of a line. Or leave out a complete line for the model to insert.

DRIVING THROUGH THE HOUSE

FUNCTION

Your model is now fully capable of moving and relocating himself. For occasions when your model refuses to move, use this activity to encourage self-propulsion.

REQUIRED ACCESSORIES

None required, but whistles, caps, and sunglasses or goggles may be used.

OPERATION

■ The user must pretend to drive a host of vehicles—for example, a car. Begin by explaining, "Get in! We're going for a ride to the kitchen." Pretend to open the "door" and help the model enter the "car." Close the door, start the ignition, and drive to the next room. Honk the horn at oncoming traffic. Drive anywhere you like in this pretend vehicle, both around the house and outside of it. Next time, the user can drive a pretend train. Call, "Choo, choo, all aboard," sound the train whistle, and commence the journey. The next trip can be on a pretend airplane. The user may even wish to depart for the journey on a bicycle built for two.

■ **NOTE:** This activity is especially useful if the model does not want to go somewhere, such as to bed or to the doctor.

SEE AND SAY

FUNCTION

During this age range, your unit's vocal sensors will expand from recognizing some twenty words to nearly one hundred. This activity will reinforce the model's understanding of basic vocabulary words.

REQUIRED ACCESSORIES

No special items required. One benefit of this activity is that it can be performed virtually anywhere.

OPERATION

■ This is a point and talk activity, with the user pointing and the unit responding. Point to things around the room, and ask the unit to name them.

VARIATIONS

Once the unit has mastered basic objects, try abstract concepts. Ask her to name something that is not visible at the moment, such as what she ate for breakfast. Discuss emotions. For example, the user can frown while asking, "How do I feel?"

CAUTION

Don't push the unit beyond her abilities. If the unit cannot name something, use the example as a teaching experience. Tell her the word she doesn't know, and repeat it gently several times.

PUDDLE JUMPER

FUNCTION

To encourage jumping, a harmless and appealing exercise activity. This activity simulates the pleasure of a rainy day but in an interior location without the mess.

REQUIRED ACCESSORIES

Several sheets of construction paper, scissors.

OPERATION

■ Prepare for the activity ahead of time by cutting several "puddles" out of the construction paper (Fig. A). Place the puddles around a room at a short distance from each other. To heighten the realism of this simulation, apply a waterproof raincoat to the model's exterior (Fig. B). Encourage the model to jump from puddle to puddle (Fig. C).

■ *NOTE:* If floor surface is slippery, user may wish to adhere "puddles" with masking tape.

VARIATIONS

Add a color recognition element. Challenge the model to jump from one puddle to a second puddle of a specific color, or to jump, for example, only on red puddles or blue puddles.

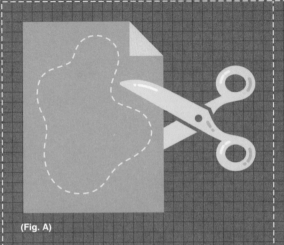

(Fig. A)

(Fig. B)

(Fig. C)

Once puddles are in place, the model will initiate self-propelled launching.

MAKE-BELIEVE ZOO

FUNCTION

The model will enjoy learning to move her body in unexpected ways. This activity also encourages the model to output new (and loud) vocal expressions.

REQUIRED ACCESSORIES

None.

OPERATION

■ Activate your model's imagination by announcing a make-believe trip to the zoo. As you begin to describe the animals, you and your model can act them out, complete with body motions and sounds. Imitate a giraffe stretching his long neck to eat a leaf. Pretend to be an elephant lifting his trunk and trumpeting out a loud call. Act like a jumpy monkey or a hungrily roaring lion. As you pretend to look in each cage, make your model feel as if she is seeing each animal and then acting like this animal.

TELEPHONE CALL

FUNCTION

Your unit is programmed for extreme language acquisition at this stage. Stimulation of this function by use of game playing is highly encouraged.

REQUIRED ACCESSORIES

Toy telephone or disabled real telephone.

OPERATION

■ Say, "Ring, ring," or otherwise simulate the sound of a ringing telephone. Explain to the model what the sound is, and what must be done to respond. Say something like, "Oh, the telephone is ringing. Let's see who it is!" Pick up or open the toy telephone. Simulate a conversation with an imaginary person on the other end. Say something like, "Hello? (Insert model name here)? Yes, he's here. Would you like to speak to him?"

■ Hand telephone to the model and encourage him to have a pretend conversation. The user can pretend to be the person on the other line by talking to the model and asking questions.

■ This information exchange can be repeated again and again. Have the model receive calls from a variety of people: parents, grandparents, friends, even his favorite animated characters.

PLAYING CATCH

FUNCTION

To exercise the catching function, whereby the model receives objects that are thrown to her. This skill will have lifelong application but must be acquired slowly and in stages.

REQUIRED ACCESSORIES

A ball that is soft and large enough that the model's hands can successfully grab it.

OPERATION

■ You may begin this activity with the model either seated or standing and facing the user. Hold the ball up to show the model. Simulate the throwing motion, and demonstrate the arc of the ball, and how it will land in the model's hands. For your first "real" throw, stand very close to the model and throw the ball a short distance. Be sure to aim at her hands, not near her face. Guide the ball into the model's hands. If the model succeeds, gradually increase the distance of the throw.

■ At the end of each throw, the model may engage an automatic repeat request; repeat activity until you determine that the model requires battery recharging. It is recommended that you practice this activity frequently, even on a daily basis.

VARIATION

If two users are available, the second user may stand behind the model and reach his or her hands around to assist with catching.

RIGHT NAME, WRONG NAME

FUNCTION

To help master label application—that is, learning to put the correct names to common objects in the world. Emphasize this skill by making purposeful and amusing mistakes.

REQUIRED ACCESSORIES

Everyday objects you use and handle regularly.

OPERATION

■ Purposely use the wrong word for things, making sure to keep your tone of voice playful and a smile visible. Hand the model a piece of bread and say, "Here's your banana." After a brief moment of perplexity, he will laugh. Older models with more advanced language skills will correct you with information already stored in their own memory files: "No, that's bread!" This activity reinforces the model's ability to name objects correctly. It also enhances his developing sense of humor, as he learns to recognize a joke.

■ Play this game on occasion for fun and education. Ask, "Would you like a book?" as you hand the model a shoe. Say, "Time for dinner!" as you put him in the bathtub. Laugh along with him when he corrects you.

■ *NOTE:* This activity also has a useful memory-check function, enabling the user to determine how much model memory is in use and which entries are in storage.

 CAUTION It's good to know when enough is enough. Play the game for fun, not to intentionally confuse the model.

MAGAZINE READER

FUNCTION

Expand application of your model's language acquisition skills. This activity will also heighten your model's ability to pair visuals with the appropriate label.

REQUIRED ACCESSORIES

A child-friendly magazine. Models will respond especially well to parenting magazines containing photographs of very young children.

OPERATION

■ Sit side by side with the model and open a magazine. Turn the pages of the magazine together. Conduct a random survey of magazine pictures, complete with user commentary. Say, for example, "Oh, look, there's a bear! Do you see it?" Or ask the model to identify what his visual sensors are picking up. Ask the model, "What do you see in this picture?"

VARIATIONS

For more advanced models, send the model on a specific search. Ask the model to locate common objects, as in: "Can you find a picture of a shoe?" You can also challenge your model to identify more abstract things, as in: "Can you find a picture of someone smiling?"

CAUTION

It is important to select a child-friendly magazine. Using magazines like *Cosmopolitan* or *Maxim* may lead to unwanted questions.

LET'S HAVE A PARADE

FUNCTION

To enhance the unit's gross motor skills. Marching is a stimulating and playful movement that will aid in this development.

REQUIRED ACCESSORIES

Legs, a selection of musical instruments (e.g., bongo drums, maracas, tambourines) or other noisemakers (e.g., plastic container with spoon, wooden toys).

OPERATION

- Announce that it's time for a parade. Select instruments for all participants. Instruct the unit to stand behind you and say that you are leading the parade. Begin to march. You may also sing a song to give the parade a festive feel and to keep a rhythm to follow. All participants should engage their musical instruments while parading.

- You may choose to create a parade route to follow through part of your house. A circular route is ideal, as it will allow a continuous loop.

VARIATIONS

Stimulate additional motor functions by changing the activity format to a skipping parade, a dancing parade, or even a crawling parade, or by switching directions unexpectedly. Switch instruments as well. Take turns with user(s) and unit(s) filling the leader function.

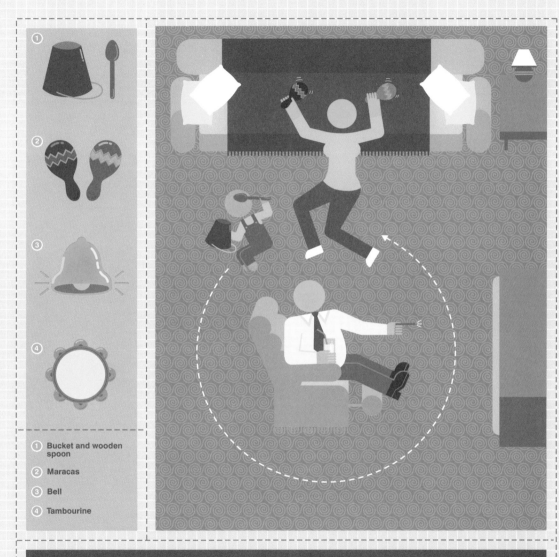

1. Bucket and wooden spoon
2. Maracas
3. Bell
4. Tambourine

Encourage every member of your household to join in the parade.

PUT A LID ON IT

FUNCTION

To heighten understanding of spatial relationships, such as the relationship of an open container to its lid.

REQUIRED ACCESSORIES

Lids and containers of various sizes and shapes. Plastic food containers, shoeboxes, pots, or any other unbreakable container with a lid will serve.

OPERATION

■ Place a selection of containers with the lids in place on a table or floor. Display this selection to the unit, and demonstrate how the lids attach and detach. After sufficient demonstration, the model should begin to replicate the user's actions by removing and replacing lids on containers.

VARIATIONS

Hide unexpected objects in several of the containers. Use toys, a small ball, or even a snack. For more advanced units, begin the game by removing the lids from all of the containers and encouraging the unit to match the appropriate lid to the correct container.

POP GOES THE BABY

FUNCTION

This simple activity utilizes the model's fascination with boxes and music.

REQUIRED ACCESSORIES

Clean, empty box large enough to contain model.

OPERATION

■ Place the model safely inside box, making sure she has enough space around her. Close flaps so that they loosely cover the top of the box. Begin to sing "Pop Goes the Weasel" (see page 130). Upon reaching the "pop!" part, open box flaps and help the model pop up and stick her head and torso out of box. Finish singing song. Reset by placing the model once again in box with lid closed, and repeat.

■ Your model is programmed to learn by imitation and repetition. Soon she will pop at the correct moment in the song, and will enjoy numerous repetitions of this activity.

WINDOW GAZER

FUNCTION

Inputting and processing data collected from the external environment.

REQUIRED ACCESSORIES

A room with a view.

OPERATION

■ Sit with unit near a window. Discuss what you see outside. See if he can point to or identify objects. Mention items you see by name, and ask him to point them out. Talk about what you see in the world outside. If people walk by, talk about what they are wearing or carrying and speculate on where they might be going.

VARIATIONS

Observe the world around you in other places, as well: in stores, out car windows, or in unfamiliar rooms in other places.

CAUTION Do not bring your model to locations where it may be exposed to extremes of temperature or other adverse conditions.

OBSTACLE COURSE

FUNCTION

Challenge the model's physical skills by creating an obstacle course. At this age, your unit will experience exponential development in her ability to manipulate her leg extensions. Her walking function will become steadier, and with her enhanced skill base, she will be able to run, jump, and turn and spin.

REQUIRED ACCESSORIES

Anything that can be moved and placed on the floor. The object(s) should be soft, solid, and free of sharp edges.

OPERATION

■ Establish perimeters and a path for the course, either indoors or in an enclosed yard with grass or other padding. Place objects at varying distances from each other. Encourage different activities and movements at each stage along the course. Arrange a pile of pillows for climbing. Assemble a pile of foam blocks to jump over. Anything can be used: a low stepstool to step onto and jump off, a plank that can serve as a balance beam, even an easel to stop and draw a picture.

■ *NOTE:* Any unexpected interference, such as falls or toppling parts, can be integrated into the obstacle course's original route.

VARIATION

Vary the course direction and course components each time.

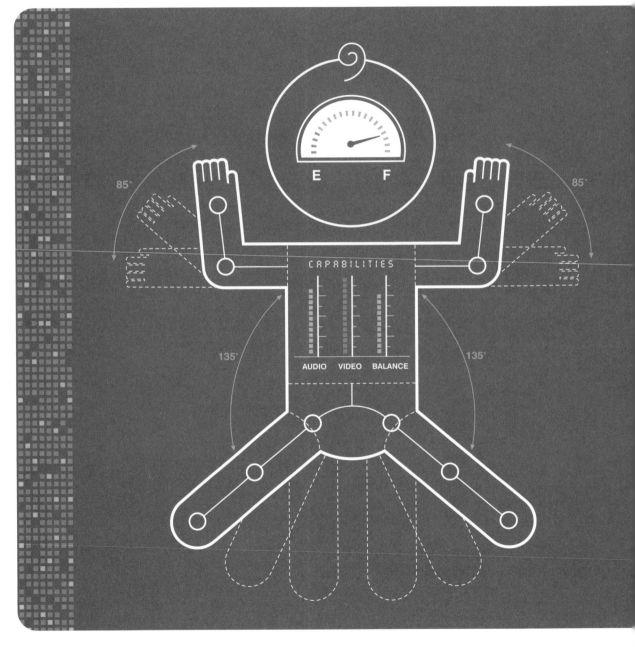

[Part 3]

25-36

MONTHS

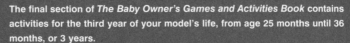

The final section of *The Baby Owner's Games and Activities Book* contains activities for the third year of your model's life, from age 25 months until 36 months, or 3 years.

During this third year of growth, your model will begin to gain some of the following abilities:

- More fluid running, jumping, skipping, and climbing, as well as ability for exploration.
- Simple storytelling and playacting.
- Faster character recognition, including letters, numbers, and shapes.
- Increased capacity of memory cache.

By this point, user and model should be quite accustomed to playing together at various activities and using this play to help develop the model's skills. Continue in this successful interactive mode.

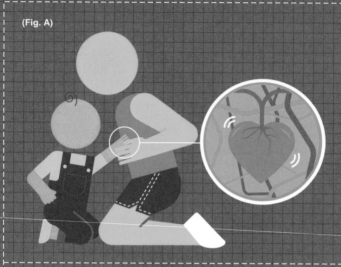

(Fig. A)

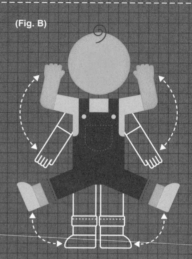

(Fig. B)

(Fig. C)

THE BEAT GOES ON

FUNCTION

Assist the model in learning about her internal features. By this age, your model will be familiar with most of her external features, so it's time to expand the range of her understanding.

REQUIRED ACCESSORIES

None.

OPERATION

■ Place the model's hand on the user's heart so the model can feel the user's heartbeat (Fig. A). Explain to the model that this is the user's heart, and that it emits regular beats. The user can mimic the heart sound vocally. Explain that the model has a heart too, and place the model's hand on her own heart. The user and model should then engage in some vigorous movement: jump up and down, run around in circles, or perform another exercise (Fig. B). Then sit again and encourage the model to feel for heartbeats (Fig. C). Point out that it is stronger and faster after movement.

VARIATION

Use a toy stethoscope (available in many play doctor kits) and pretend to take each other's heart rate.

FINGER PUPPETS

FUNCTION

Teaching the model to recognize different emotions. At this age, your model's emotional sensors will become highly sensitive to outside stimulation—he is gradually becoming aware that other people have feelings.

REQUIRED ACCESSORIES

Felt and glue. Cut felt of various colors into shapes that will fit over human fingers. Glue two same-sized pieces together to make a puppet. Create faces expressing different emotions either by gluing on smaller pieces of felt or by drawing them on with a marker. Alternatively, use the finger puppets on pages 134–135.

OPERATION

■ Introduce the puppets to the model. In a playful voice, act out each character and tell the model how the puppet is feeling.

■ The puppets' dialogue can be variations on the following script:
"Hi, I'm Fred the Dragon. I'm very happy today! I just had my favorite lunch!"
"I'm Susie the Fish. I'm sad. My brother won't play with me!"
"I'm Johnny the Tiger. I'm angry! My favorite toy just broke!"

■ Create plays with the puppets, and have them interact with the model and with each other. By observing and responding, your model will learn about how emotions are experienced and expressed.

VARIATIONS

Any toy, stuffed animal, or other object can be given a voice and made to express emotions. It can also explain the ramifications of the model's actions—ask questions like, "How do you think the puppet felt when you hit it?"

READ TO ME

FUNCTION

Assist your model in recognizing and comprehending words. These words are strings of characters that are formed by combining different letter shapes.

REQUIRED ACCESSORIES

Books, a local library.

OPERATION

■ Read to your model as often as possible—once daily or more, if possible. There is no danger of introducing reading "too early," and many users will share picture books with newborns. By the age of 25 months, however, your child will begin acquiring the skills to read for himself. Spend some time at the library reading to your model. Read different kinds of books, and take advantage of the child-friendly seating offered by many of these institutions. The user is encouraged to use a lively tone and to take advantage of her vocal range in bringing books to life by reading to the model (but be sure to maintain a vocal volume that will not disrupt other library users). Apply for a library card in the model's name, and use it to take books home to read.

VARIATIONS

Show the model how to read to himself. Even though he's probably too young to decipher words, he can still mimic the act of reading and look at the pictures. If he is reading a book that has been read to him many times, he knows the story and can tell it to himself while he is leafing through book pages. After he's finished reading a book, encourage him to draw his own picture of the story.

CHOICE CHORES

FUNCTION

Involving your model in the daily life of the household. This particular activity makes chores a playful part of the unit's daily routine.

REQUIRED ACCESSORIES

Accoutrements of the chosen chore, from silverware to a broom or mop (in child-sized versions if available).

OPERATION

■ Introduce the model to the activity by demonstrating how it is performed. Then ask the model to take a turn. Sweep the floor together (this activity is particularly rewarding for the model when a child-sized broom is used). Exaggerate sweeping motions to be more playful. Dance with the broom. Take turns sweeping different spots. Set the table together. Ask the model to assist in transporting items (preferably the nonbreakable ones) to the table and placing silverware. Walk around the table with the model and count the number of forks or spoons. Fold the laundry together and count socks. Have the model assist in making the bed: Begin by placing the model on bed and tossing the sheet on top of him, and then proceed to normal bed-making routine.

VARIATIONS

The model can be incorporated into any chore in a playful way, which will help to build a sense of involvement and responsibility.

CAUTION Keep the model away from all dangerous cleaning items, such as bleach or other harsh chemicals.

FAMILY PORTRAIT

FUNCTION

Your model is aware of his place as part of a family grouping. This activity reinforces her feelings of comfort and protection. While doing so, the user can also activate model's ability to recall and reproduce details and visual characteristics.

REQUIRED ACCESSORIES

Drawing pad, crayons, family photographs.

OPERATION

■ Discuss the members of the model's family group. This can include only parents and siblings or a wider circle including grandparents, cousins, etc. Talk about each one's notable physical characteristics: hair style and color, size, favorite clothing, and so on. Look at photographs of family members. Encourage the model to draw family members either individually or as one large group portrait.

VARIATIONS

Discuss the model's own physical characteristics. Encourage the model to draw a self-portrait.

FUN WITH HATS

FUNCTION

Encourage the model's creativity and self-expression via dress-up play.

REQUIRED ACCESSORIES

A collection of hats that can be assembled over several months and preferably stored in a dedicated bag or box. Hats can include discarded baseball caps, fedoras, and knit winter hats, as well as costume hats in kid sizes, such as pirate hats, three-cornered hats, and so forth.

OPERATION

■ Present your model with the hat collection. Together, reach in and pull out a hat for the model to wear. The user or the model should place hat on the model's head. The model (and the user too, if desired) should become whatever character is indicated by the hat, and role play can begin.

VARIATIONS

Provide additional props for more complete playacting. Introduce other models and users to the play, and make up and act out stories.

Playing with hats can prompt a model to imagine any number of fantastic situations.

PLAYING WITH DOUGH

FUNCTION

Manipulating and strengthening the model's digits and fine motor movements. This activity also encourages the development of creative artistic programming.

REQUIRED ACCESSORIES

Applesauce dough (which can be made by mixing 1 part applesauce with 1 part cinnamon). Mess-free mixing can be accomplished by combining ingredients in a sealable plastic bag and kneading the contents. Optional: cookie cutters.

OPERATION

■ Encourage your model to participate in the production of the dough. Once it exists, encourage the model to manipulate the dough and structure it into different shapes and forms. The model may also choose to use preformed shapes, such as cookie cutters, to help mold the dough. Finished designs can be left to dry and then displayed on flat surfaces such as tables and book-shelves. Or they can be attached to yarn or string and used as hanging displays. (They will also scent a room with the smell of cinnamon.)

VARIATION

Work with the model to form dough into letters and numbers.

CAUTION

Make sure any sharp objects, such as cookie cutters, are used with supervision. Also note that while the dough is edible, it is not tasty, and ingesting the dough should not be encouraged.

TREASURE CHEST, VERSION 2.0

FUNCTION

Further development of spatial relationships. Models of all ages will enjoy opening a box to discover its contents. In this activity, the objects, once removed, offer further possibilities for usage.

REQUIRED ACCESSORIES

As with the treasure chest described in Version 1.0 (page 41), choose a sturdy and visually appealing container with a lid. Fill it with a selection of items for the model to discover, including small toys and games and arts and crafts materials.

OPERATION

■ Present treasure chest to the model. Encourage the model to open the box and begin to remove contents. Do not rush through contents, but rather stop and see what each item in the box might offer. For example, if the model discovers a package of felt and a bottle of glue, you may decide to make finger puppets (see pages 134–135). Other art objects (such as paints, glue, pens, or markers) could lead to additional activities. Be sure to include a small book to read together or a family photograph to discuss. Place some dolls or small cars and trucks in the box, or a harmonica, flute, or small drum, and take time to play separately with each item. When finished, replace all items and close lid, leaving all contents intact for the next usage.

VARIATIONS

The next time you run this activity, add some new contents. Or, have the model close his eyes while picking out an item.

(Fig. A)

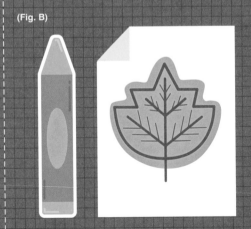

(Fig. B)

(Fig. C)

LEAF IT TO ME

FUNCTION

Develop sensory perceptiveness by engaging in activities related to the changing seasons.

REQUIRED ACCESSORIES

Autumn conditions of changing and falling leaves, a bag for collecting.

OPERATION

■ Take your model on an outdoor excursion with the goal of focusing on leaves. Point out the changing leaves on the trees and note color variations, thus exercising her visual sensors. Encourage the model to hunt for fallen leaves and fill the bag with favored choices. Alternatively, you can find or make a pile of leaves, and encourage the model to jump or play in the pile (Fig. A). This will engage her touch sensors and enhance gross motor skills.

■ Continue leaf play indoors with the leaves you have collected in the bag. Make art projects by pasting them to paper or using them as stencils and tracing them with crayons on construction paper (Fig. B). The user may also create a leaf pathway indoors for model to follow (Fig. C).

SHAPE HUNT

FUNCTION

Reinforcing shape identification. At this age, your model will be highly aware of shapes and boundaries.

REQUIRED ACCESSORIES

Paper and crayons or markers.

OPERATION

- Begin this activity by displaying a shape, such as a circle, square, triangle, or rectangle. The user can display this shape either by providing an item (such as a block) that features the shape, or by drawing a representation of the shape on paper. This will enable the model to identify and name the shape. Follow this by helping the model to draw the shape. Next, go on a shape hunt, either in the home or in the external environment. Seek out the shape under discussion. Count how many are discovered.

VARIATION

Numbers and letters can be substituted for shapes.

HIDE AND SEEK

FUNCTION

Further development of object permanence. At this age, your model will certainly understand that the user is still present or nearby even if the user's entire body is not currently visible.

REQUIRED ACCESSORIES

Immobile objects, such as doors, beds, trees, etc.

OPERATION

■ The user should challenge the model: "Come and find me!" The user should then hide behind a large nearby object (see Required Accessories list), perhaps leaving a tiny bit of her body still visible. The user can call to the model, giving vocal clues as to her whereabouts (or, most likely, the model will have watched the user hide and will know where to find her).

■ Next, reverse the game and encourage the model to hide. As the user seeks the model, describe the search aloud for the model's pleasure, as in: "Where is [model's name]? I'm looking in the bedroom, but I don't see [model's name]! Where could he be?" Having not completely grasped the concept of the game, the model may announce his location ahead of time (as in: "I'm hiding behind the shower curtain, Mommy—come find me!"), or, upon being discovered, may ask for a "replay" (as in: "Pretend you didn't find me, Mommy—look again!"). As with many other activities, this game may evolve into a continuous loop.

CAUTION Don't hide, and don't allow the model to hide, in any dangerous places, such as closets or cabinets where doors could accidentally lock.

PARTY TIME

FUNCTION

Encouraging your model to interact with other models. Most of the activities in this manual are designed for the user and model exclusively; this activity is geared toward socialization that will become critical at a later age.

REQUIRED ACCESSORIES

Other compatible models of similar age.

OPERATION

- Bring models together in a playroom with toys and games available. Once they seem comfortable in one another's presence, introduce some basic interactive programming. Gather models standing in a circle holding hands and have them go round and round to music, or have them be seated and clap along to the music. Arrange models in pairs to play age-appropriate board games or to play with train sets or other interactive toys. Encourage sharing and taking turns.

CAUTION

Approach this activity with expectations of only limited interaction. Models of this age often pursue what is referred to as _parallel play_, where two or more models play side by side rather than directly with each other.

FAMILY HISTORY

FUNCTION

Your unit's memory capacity is constantly expanding, and her random access memory contains records of past events. Access your model's memory cache by creating stories based on past activities.

REQUIRED ACCESSORIES

Create finger puppets by pasting cut-out photos of family members and friends on Popsicle sticks or tongue depressors. Laminate photos before attaching if desired.

OPERATION

■ Introduce your model to the puppet figures. Begin to tell a story. Base the story on something the model has done recently, such as a trip to the zoo or even the supermarket. Bring in different puppets at different parts of the story. Let the model hold the puppets and participate in storytelling.

VARIATIONS

Use at bedtime to review and reinforce the day's activities. Or create entirely new adventures and stories.

CAVE DWELLER

FUNCTION

Your model will be constantly improving her ability to identify and name objects. Use this activity as another way to hone that skill.

REQUIRED ACCESSORIES

A small enclosed space; pictures of animals, either drawn or cut from magazines or out of construction paper; masking tape.

OPERATION

■ Create a pretend cave in a large box or a small room. Tape pictures of animals to the walls. Darken the space, and equip the model with a flashlight. Bring model into said space and program the model into seek mode by instructing her to use the flashlight beam to pick out various animals in the dark. Name the animals one at a time, and ask the model to locate and identify them. Once all the animals have been located, turn on the lights to reveal the entire array.

! CAUTION Never leave the model alone in a dark enclosed space.

(Fig. A)

BUBBALOO

(Fig. B)

(Fig. C)

POP!

Chasing bubbles is an excellent way to increase a unit's hand-eye coordination.

BUBBLE FUN

FUNCTION

Developing hand/eye coordination via bubble-blowing. This simple activity can be endlessly entertaining for both model and user. Your model has a built-in inclination to chase and pop these shiny buoyant objects.

REQUIRED ACCESSORIES

Bottle of bubble liquid, bubble wands of any shape and size (Fig. A).

OPERATION

■ Choose a location (preferably outdoors) where the user can perch and blow bubbles into a space where the model can watch and chase them. Or hand the wand to the model and encourage your model to blow some bubbles (Fig. B) and then pop as many bubbles as possible with his fingers (Fig. C). After the model has successfully engaged in sequential finger-popping, specify other body parts to be used for bubble popping: elbows, knees, noses, etc. This adds an anatomy lesson to the exercise.

■ After this activity, wipe your model with a soft damp cloth. Do not use any harsh solvents.

VARIATION

In recent years, "catchable" bubble solution has entered the marketplace. This unique product creates bubbles that will last several minutes before collapsing.

PAINT WITH WATER

FUNCTION

This activity stimulates development of the model's imagination and motor skills. Depending on your success, it may also cause your model to smile.

REQUIRED ACCESSORIES

A bucket filled with warm water (Fig. A), and a paintbrush (preferably the kind used for wall painting, with a wide brush and a large handle). Real paint is not recommended for this activity.

OPERATION

■ Arrange the model, bucket, and paintbrush in an outdoor location with ample traffic-free concrete (not blacktop) surface, such as a sidewalk. Submerge the paintbrush in the water (Fig. B), then use it to "paint" designs on the concrete. Repeat several times until your model reaches to take the paintbrush.

■ For faster results, use two paintbrushes (Fig. C). Place one in the model's hand at the commencement of the activity. The user should then proceed as described above. After a short time, the model should begin to simulate user movements.

■ The educational benefits of this procedure can be expanded by "painting" and naming letters, numbers, or shapes. Or you can draw pictures and command your unit to identify them.

VARIATIONS

Add bubbles or food coloring to water. For a winter version of this activity, equip the model with a spray bottle filled with water and food coloring; the model can spraypaint the snow

CAUTION

Never place or store an unprotected unit in direct sunlight for extended periods of time. If activity takes place on a sunny day, be sure to adequately coat the model's exposed surfaces with a child-safe sunscreen.

(Fig. A)

(Fig. B)

(Fig. C)

Depending on outdoor temperatures, artwork will evaporate within 5–15 minutes,
at which point you can encourage the model to begin again.

MONKEY SEE, MONKEY DO

FUNCTION

Teaching any number of new skills to the model. At this age, your model will be constantly acquiring new physical skills. Follow the leader–type games encourage new skill initialization.

REQUIRED ACCESSORIES

None required, but any sort of toy or prop can be utilized.

OPERATION

■ Stand in front of the model and offer a playful challenge such as "Can you do this?" or "Follow me!" Perform a movement for model to replicate. Touch your nose with your finger. Again, say, "Look at me! Can you do this?" Make sure this activity is made to feel playful. Repeat until the model mimics user movements.

■ Once your model is trained to imitate your actions, you can introduce countless additional simple movements. Hop on one foot. Run in a serpentine shape. Jump and pat your head. Spin in a circle. These activities will challenge your model's growing physical dexterity in a positive and encouraging way.

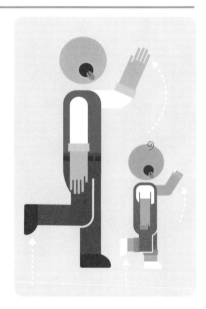

SORTING OBJECTS

FUNCTION

Your model can discern identifying characteristics of different objects; she can also tell which objects are similar and which are not alike. This activity hones this ability.

REQUIRED ACCESSORIES

A variety of small objects, with multiples of each kind; muffin tin or other container with six or more separate sections.

OPERATION

■ Place one of each small object in each compartment of the muffin tin. Place the tin in front of the model. Hand the model a cup or other container containing the rest of the objects all mixed together. The objective is for the model to sort all of the objects, and to place each one in the section of the tin with like objects.

VARIATIONS

Place three of one item on a table, and one different item. Have model select the object that is different than the others.

CAUTION The model must never insert any of these objects into her oral cavity.

RHYME TIME

FUNCTION

Stimulating synaptic development via the use of rhyming words and language patterns.

REQUIRED ACCESSORIES

User language skills.

OPERATION

■ Quote a short poem or make up a sentence that utilizes simple rhymes. For example, "Look, I see, there's a tree." The user can announce, "That rhymes!" and repeat the rhyming words to explain and emphasize: "See, tree." Then the user can make a game of it, as in: "Let's think of other words that rhyme with see." User(s) and model continue the activity by playing with an entire range of words and rhymes.

BEAN ME UP

FUNCTION

Encouraging the manipulation of materials and use of the model's grasping functions, as well as other fine motor skills.

REQUIRED ACCESSORIES

Bucket, pail, or bowl filled with uncooked beans, rice, peas, sand, or other small particles; table, towel or sheet for underneath layer; shovels or small empty containers for scoops.

OPERATION

■ Place your model in proximity to the arrangement of accessories. Encourage play. The model can engage material in any number of ways. The model can spill contents onto floor or table, spread them about, pile them, etc. The model can pour from one bucket to another (it is helpful to have a second large container on hand). The model can thrust his hand extensions into the bucket and swish the beans about. The model will enjoy endless play with these simple organic materials.

VARIATIONS

The unit can engage in similarly modeled play in other locales, such as at the beach with sand, in the tub with water, or outdoors with snow. The user may also wish to hide small objects or toys in the beans for the model to discover.

 CAUTION The model must never insert any of these objects into his oral cavity.

JUMP TO IT

FUNCTION

Encouraging the jumping function in controlled settings. At this age, your model can easily jump from steps and chairs, and likely enjoys launching herself this way.

REQUIRED ACCESSORIES

Local furniture and immobile objects such as steps.

OPERATION

■ Turn a walk into an opportunity for jumping. Instead of walking into another room, or taking a walk around the block, take a jump—and encourage the model to jump from place to place. Set up small practice areas for jumping, such as from a low, solid bench or stool, or from a bottom step of a staircase. Make a course of pillows, paper, or other flat objects, and have the model jump from one to the next. All this jumping is an excellent way for model to utilize gross motor skills and expel excess energy.

VARIATIONS

Initiate other unexpected or uncommon methods of getting from A to B: hopping, walking backwards, or even the now-obsolete crawling function.

CAUTION

Never allow the model to jump from any height unattended; factory warranties do not cover damage caused by this activity.

COUNT ME IN

FUNCTION

Encourages counting and quantifying objects. Fingers and toes are perfect tools for counting. The user can also incorporate counting into other activities around the house, such as walking from room to room.

REQUIRED ACCESSORIES

None.

OPERATION

The user should begin this activity by initiating basic counting exercises. Together with the model, count to ten. Then count to twenty. Then stand together, and announce that you are going to measure the room in steps. Walk together from one end of the room to the other, counting each step aloud as you walk. In this way, you can measure any room and turn walking from here to there into a counting exercise.

VARIATION

Count frequently recurring objects in the home: windows, doors, chairs, etc.

WHY ASK WHY?

FUNCTION

As your model's command center retains more and more information, it will simultaneously require a more detailed understanding of the things it encounters. This need is manifested by extremely frequent use of the one-word question "Why?"

REQUIRED ACCESSORIES

User patience.

OPERATION

■ Treat the model's questions with consideration. Let the model see that you are paying attention to him, and that you are listening carefully to his inquiry. Then turn this question back around to the model, and use it to provoke the model to perform additional self-generated processing.

■ When the model asks "Why?" respond by asking, "Why do you think?" After repetition of this technique, the model will realize you are not merely going to provide him with all the answers.

■ Follow up your return question with some more specific questions designed to point toward figuring out the answer. Say: "Do you think it is because [put a possible answer here]?" or "Is it because X or Y, do you think?"

■ This way of responding to the perpetual "Why" changes the model's continous loop into a bit of a game and an opportunity for user and model to simultaneously acquire knowledge.

VARIATION

On occasion, when in doubt, an old-fashioned "Because I said so" can still be safely employed by the user.

DRESS REHEARSAL

FUNCTION

While every attempt has been made to provide your model with an outer covering that is both visually appealing and climate-resistant, it is essential to carefully protect this covering from climatic fluctuations. The user must carefully apply appropriate clothing on the model. However, since models are programmed to eventually achieve self-sufficiency, the user must also train the model to apply coverings herself.

REQUIRED ACCESSORIES

Weather-appropriate garments of correct size.

OPERATION

■ Prepare the model for independent implementation of this activity by describing elements of clothing while dressing her. Say to the model, for example, "Now I'm putting on your pants. First we put in one leg, and then the other."

■ Then encourage the model to dress herself. Lay clothes out flat on floor, and seat the model next to them. Ask the model to attempt the dressing procedure. This can be done in several ways:
1. As a cheerful invitation, as in: "Guess what? Today you get to get dressed all by yourself!"
2. As a challenge, either positive or negative: "Can you get dressed all by yourself?" or "I bet you can't put your clothes on all by yourself!"
3. As a race: "How fast can you put on your shirt? I'm going to count . . ." This is especially effective if there is an older sibling present against whom to race.

■ Model will require assistance in the early stages of this activity but will eventually be able to achieve full clothing coverage independently. Celebrate their success when the goal is attained.

MYSTERY BAG

FUNCTION

Additional development of object identification. This variation places emphasis on touch sensors.

REQUIRED ACCESSORIES

Selection of small- to medium-sized objects with protruding parts and identifiable outlines. Frequently used familiar toys are recommended. A medium-sized nontransparent bag, preferably drawstring.

OPERATION

■ Place a small selection of items in the bag (or the user can insert items one at a time). Instruct the model to reach into the bag, grab one item, and, without removing his hand from the bag, feel the item carefully. The model is to try to identify the item based on what he can feel. If needed, the user can supply verbal clues to assist the model in guessing.

VARIATIONS

The same activity can be done by placing a blindfold on the model and placing the mystery object on a table in front of the model. This way the model can use two hands to feel object.

CAUTION

Do not use any items with sharp parts.

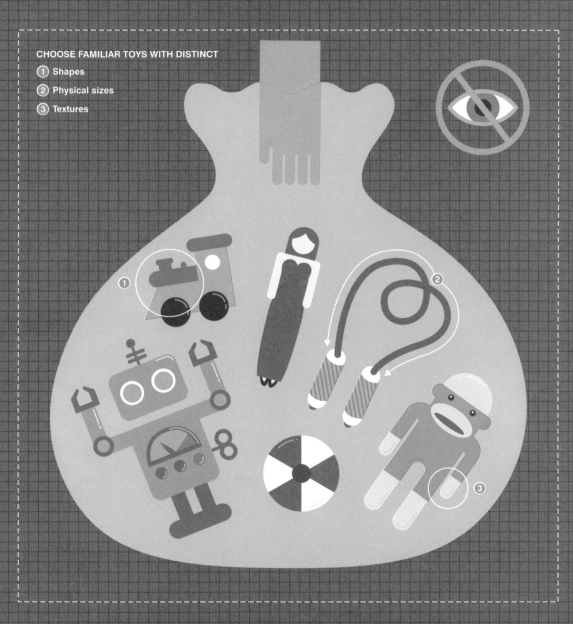

CHOOSE FAMILIAR TOYS WITH DISTINCT

① Shapes

② Physical sizes

③ Textures

APPENDIX

Useful Materials

Your model is fitted for compatibility with many attachments and accessories. For the advanced activities contained in this manual, it will be helpful to keep the following items on hand:

- A mobile with dangling black and white graphic designs.
- Individual toys with black and white graphic designs.
- A music player or players—CD player, radio, etc.—along with music source such as CDs or cassette tapes.
- A soft mat, towel, or blanket suitable for placing model on top of floor.
- Small child-safe handheld toys such as rattles and stuffed animals.
- Mirrors of different sizes: a full-length mirror hung on a wall as well as smaller handheld mirrors. Plastic or other child-proof mirrors of unbreakable materials that can be placed in crib or model play space are useful.
- Soft, clean feather, preferably of the germ-free synthetic variety.
- Colorful ribbons or streamers.
- Sheer oblong scarf.
- Balls of different sizes and weights.
- Pots, pans, or other kitchen containers and their lids.
- Empty plastic containers, with and without lids.
- Empty and clean cardboard box of size larger than the model.
- Clean, empty cartons leftover from orange juice, milk, etc.

- Cornstarch.

- Food coloring.

- Applesauce and cinnamon.

- Large paper or drawing pad and extra thick crayons and markers.

- Construction paper.

- Masking tape.

- Immersible water toys.

- Blocks and tiles with letters on them.

- Shaving cream.

- Toy whistles.

- Child-sized sunglasses.

- Toy telephone or disabled real telephone.

- Books and magazines.

- A selection of musical instruments, child and/or adult-sized.

- Felt and glue.

- A collection of assorted hats.

- Popsicle or craft sticks.

- Bottle of bubble liquid and bubble wands of any shape or size.

- A paintbrush (preferably the kind used for wall painting, with a wide brush and a large handle).

■ Muffin tin or other container with six or more separate sections.

■ A selection of small objects, with multiples of each kind.

■ Bucket, pail, or bowl.

■ Uncooked beans, rice, peas.

■ Sand.

■ A medium-sized nontransparent bag, preferably drawstring.

In the process of implementing the activities in this manual, the user will also develop auxiliary activities. The user should feel free to improvise and create, and in doing so, the user should discover that developing programming for the model is not complicated and does not require specialized training. For future activities, consider having some of the following items available in the model's living environment:

■ Arts and crafts items in addition to those listed above, such as paint, child-safe scissors, glitter glue, and stickers.

■ Dress-up items, including old clothing and shoes, jewelry, scarves, purses, etc.

■ Food-related items, such as flour, salt, and liquid starch, that can be used for play and to make other substances.

■ Household cleaning items in miniature sizes, such as brooms, and toy replicas of these items, such as toy vacuum cleaners and lawnmowers.

■ Books, including typical childhood stories and nursery rhymes.

■ Common household items like empty paper towel rolls and empty large cartons and boxes.

■ A selection of toys with moveable parts (but not small parts that risk being swallowed).

SONGS AND RHYMES

SEVERAL OF THE ACTIVITIES IN THIS MANUAL SUGGEST THAT THE USER SING SONGS TO ACCOMPANY THE ACTIVITY. FOLLOWING ARE THE LYRICS TO SOME FAVORITE NURSERY RHYMES AND OTHER CHILDREN'S SONGS.

BAA, BAA, BLACK SHEEP

BAA, BAA, BLACK SHEEP, HAVE YOU ANY WOOL?

YES, SIR, YES, SIR, THREE BAGS FULL.

ONE FOR MY MASTER, ONE FOR MY DAME,

AND ONE FOR THE LITTLE BOY WHO LIVES DOWN THE LANE.

BAA, BAA, BLACK SHEEP, HAVE YOU ANY WOOL?

YES, SIR, YES, SIR, THREE BAGS FULL.

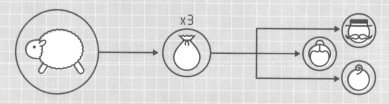

ITSY BITSY SPIDER

THE ITSY BITSY SPIDER CLIMBED UP THE WATERSPOUT.

DOWN CAME THE RAIN, AND WASHED THE SPIDER OUT.

OUT CAME THE SUN AND DRIED UP ALL THE RAIN,

AND THE ITSY BITSY SPIDER CLIMBED UP THE SPOUT AGAIN.

THE ITSY BITSY SPIDER CLIMBED UP THE KITCHEN WALL.

SWOOSH! WENT THE FAN, AND MADE THE SPIDER FALL.

OFF WENT THE FAN, NO LONGER DID IT BLOW,

SO THE ITSY BITSY SPIDER BACK UP THE WALL DID GO.

THE ITSY BITSY SPIDER CLIMBED UP THE YELLOW PAIL.

IN CAME A MOUSE, AND FLICKED HER WITH HIS TAIL.

DOWN FELL THE SPIDER, THE MOUSE RAN OUT THE DOOR,

THEN THE ITSY BITSY SPIDER CLIMBED UP THE PAIL ONCE MORE.

THE ITSY BITSY SPIDER CLIMBED UP THE ROCKING CHAIR.

UP JUMPED A CAT, AND KNOCKED HER IN THE AIR.

DOWN PLOPPED THE CAT, AND WHEN HE WAS ASLEEP,

THE ITSY BITSY SPIDER BACK UP THE CHAIR DID CREEP.

THE ITSY BITSY SPIDER CLIMBED UP THE MAPLE TREE.

SHE SLIPPED ON SOME DEW AND LANDED NEXT TO ME.

OUT CAME THE SUN, AND WHEN THE TREE WAS DRY,

THE ITSY BITSY SPIDER GAVE IT ONE MORE TRY.

THE ITSY BITSY SPIDER CLIMBED UP WITHOUT A STOP.

SHE SPUN A SILKY WEB RIGHT AT THE VERY TOP.

SHE WOVE AND SHE SPUN, AND WHEN HER WEB WAS DONE,

THE ITSY BITSY SPIDER RESTED IN THE SUN.

I'VE BEEN WORKING ON THE RAILROAD

I'VE BEEN WORKIN' ON THE RAILROAD, ALL THE LIVE-LONG DAY.

I'VE BEEN WORKIN' ON THE RAILROAD, JUST TO PASS THE TIME AWAY.

DON'T YOU HEAR THE WHISTLE BLOWING? RISE UP SO EARLY IN THE MORN.

DON'T YOU HEAR THE CAPTAIN SHOUTING, "DINAH, BLOW YOUR HORN"?

DINAH, WON'T YOU BLOW, DINAH, WON'T YOU BLOW, DINAH, WON'T YOU BLOW YOUR HORN? (x2)

SOMEONE'S IN THE KITCHEN WITH DINAH, SOMEONE'S IN THE KITCHEN, I KNOW.

SOMEONE'S IN THE KITCHEN WITH DINAH, STRUMMING ON THE OLD BANJO.

AND SINGIN' FEE, FIE, FIDDLE-E-I-O. FEE, FIE, FIDDLE-E-I-O-O-O-O.

FEE, FIE, FIDDLE-E-I-O. STRUMMING ON THE OLD BANJO.

MY BONNIE LIES OVER THE OCEAN

MY BONNIE LIES OVER THE OCEAN, MY BONNIE LIES OVER THE SEA.

MY BONNIE LIES OVER THE OCEAN, PLEASE BRING BACK MY BONNIE TO ME.

BRING BACK, BRING BACK, OH, BRING BACK MY BONNIE TO ME, TO ME. (x2)

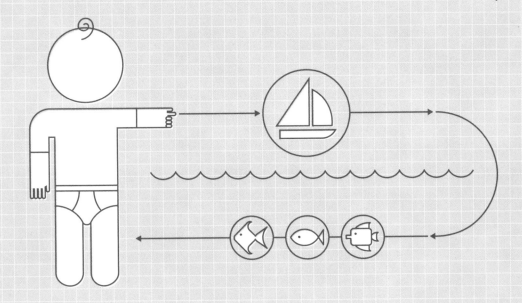

OH, DEAR, WHAT CAN THE MATTER BE

OH, DEAR, WHAT CAN THE MATTER BE? DEAR, DEAR, WHAT CAN THE MATTER BE?

OH, DEAR, WHAT CAN THE MATTER BE? JOHNNY'S SO LONG AT THE FAIR.

HE PROMISED TO BUY ME A BUNCH OF BLUE RIBBONS;

HE PROMISED TO BUY ME SOME BONNY BLUE RIBBONS;

HE PROMISED TO BUY ME A BUNCH OF BLUE RIBBONS, TO BIND UP MY BONNY BROWN HAIR.

AND IT'S, OH! DEAR! WHAT CAN THE MATTER BE? DEAR, DEAR, WHAT CAN THE MATTER BE?

OH, DEAR, WHAT CAN THE MATTER BE? JOHNNY'S SO LONG AT THE FAIR.

OH, SUSANNA

I COME FROM ALABAMA WITH MY BANJO ON MY KNEE.

I'M GOIN' TO LOUISIANA MY TRUE LOVE FOR TO SEE;

IT RAINED ALL NIGHT THE DAY I LEFT, THE WEATHER IT WAS DRY;

THE SUN SO HOT I FROZE TO DEATH; SUSANNA, DON'T YOU CRY.

OH, SUSANNA, OH, DON'T YOU CRY FOR ME,

I'VE COME FROM ALABAMA WITH MY BANJO ON MY KNEE.

OH, SUSANNA, OH, DON'T YOU CRY FOR ME,

'CAUSE I'M GOIN' TO LOUISIANA, MY TRUE LOVE FOR TO SEE.

I HAD A DREAM THE OTHER NIGHT WHEN EV'RYTHING WAS STILL;

I THOUGHT I SAW SUSANNA A-COMIN' DOWN THE HILL;

THE BUCKWHEAT CAKE WAS IN HER MOUTH, THE TEAR WAS IN HER EYE;

SAYS I, I'M COMIN' FROM THE SOUTH, SUSANNA, DON'T YOU CRY.

OH, SUSANNA, OH, DON'T YOU CRY FOR ME,

I'VE COME FROM ALABAMA WITH MY BANJO ON MY KNEE.

OH, SUSANNA, OH, DON'T YOU CRY FOR ME,

'CAUSE I'M GOIN' TO LOUISIANA, MY TRUE LOVE FOR TO SEE.

OLD MACDONALD HAD A FARM

OLD MACDONALD HAD A FARM, E-I-E-I-O.

AND ON HIS FARM HE HAD A COW, E-I-E-I-O.

WITH A MOO, MOO HERE AND A MOO, MOO THERE,

HERE A MOO, THERE A MOO, EVERYWHERE A MOO-MOO,

OLD MACDONALD HAD A FARM, E-I-E-I-O.

Repeat verse for each of the other farm animals, substituting
COW with the animal's name and MOO with its respective sound:

PIG	HORSE	SHEEP	CHICKEN	DOG
"OINK"	"NEIGH"	"BAA"	"CLUCK"	"BOW WOW"

POP GOES THE WEASEL

ALL AROUND THE MULBERRY BUSH, THE MONKEY CHASED THE WEASEL.

THE MONKEY THOUGHT 'TWAS ALL IN FUN. POP! GOES THE WEASEL.

A PENNY FOR A SPOOL OF THREAD, A PENNY FOR A NEEDLE.

THAT'S THE WAY THE MONEY GOES. POP! GOES THE WEASEL.

UP AND DOWN THE CITY ROAD, IN AND OUT OF THE EAGLE.

THAT'S THE WAY THE MONEY GOES. POP! GOES THE WEASEL.

HALF A POUND OF TWOPENNY RICE, HALF A POUND OF TREACLE.

MIX IT UP AND MAKE IT NICE, POP! GOES THE WEASEL.

THIS LITTLE PIGGY

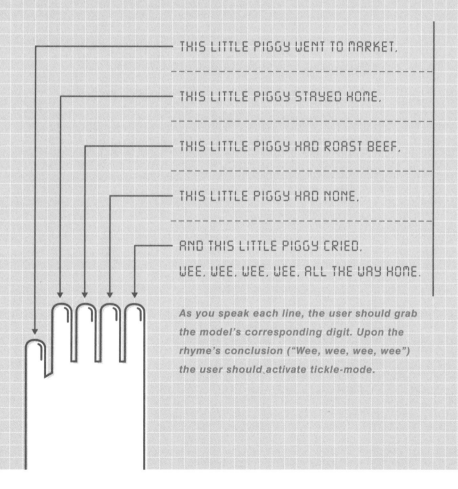

THIS LITTLE PIGGY WENT TO MARKET.

THIS LITTLE PIGGY STAYED HOME.

THIS LITTLE PIGGY HAD ROAST BEEF.

THIS LITTLE PIGGY HAD NONE.

AND THIS LITTLE PIGGY CRIED.
WEE. WEE. WEE. WEE. ALL THE WAY HOME.

As you speak each line, the user should grab the model's corresponding digit. Upon the rhyme's conclusion ("Wee, wee, wee, wee") the user should activate tickle-mode.

TWINKLE, TWINKLE, LITTLE STAR,

HOW I WONDER WHAT YOU ARE.

UP ABOVE THE WORLD SO HIGH,

LIKE A DIAMOND IN THE SKY.

TWINKLE, TWINKLE, LITTLE STAR,

HOW I WONDER WHAT YOU ARE.

PUPPET FACES

THE FOLLOWING PAGES CONTAIN FACES TO BE CUT OUT AND USED WITH THE FINGER PUPPETS ACTIVITY FOUND ON PAGE 84. BABY OWNERS MAY WISH TO MAKE PHOTOCOPIES OF EACH FACE AND THEN DRAW A DIFFERENT EMOTIONAL SIGNAL ON EACH ONE.

Log of Favorite Activities

DATE	ACTIVITY	COMMENTS
☐☐ / ☐☐ Month Day		
☐☐ / ☐☐ Month Day		
☐☐ / ☐☐ Month Day		
☐☐ / ☐☐ Month Day		
☐☐ / ☐☐ Month Day		
☐☐ / ☐☐ Month Day		
☐☐ / ☐☐ Month Day		
☐☐ / ☐☐ Month Day		

Log of Favorite Activities

DATE	ACTIVITY	COMMENTS
☐☐ / ☐☐ Month Day		
☐☐ / ☐☐ Month Day		
☐☐ / ☐☐ Month Day		
☐☐ / ☐☐ Month Day		
☐☐ / ☐☐ Month Day		
☐☐ / ☐☐ Month Day		
☐☐ / ☐☐ Month Day		
☐☐ / ☐☐ Month Day		

Log of Favorite Activities

DATE	ACTIVITY	COMMENTS
☐☐ / ☐☐ Month Day		
☐☐ / ☐☐ Month Day		
☐☐ / ☐☐ Month Day		
☐☐ / ☐☐ Month Day		
☐☐ / ☐☐ Month Day		
☐☐ / ☐☐ Month Day		
☐☐ / ☐☐ Month Day		
☐☐ / ☐☐ Month Day		

Log of Favorite Activities

DATE	ACTIVITY	COMMENTS
Month / Day		
Month / Day		
Month / Day		
Month / Day		
Month / Day		
Month / Day		
Month / Day		
Month / Day		

Log of Favorite Activities

DATE	ACTIVITY	COMMENTS
☐☐ / ☐☐ Month Day		
☐☐ / ☐☐ Month Day		
☐☐ / ☐☐ Month Day		
☐☐ / ☐☐ Month Day		
☐☐ / ☐☐ Month Day		
☐☐ / ☐☐ Month Day		
☐☐ / ☐☐ Month Day		
☐☐ / ☐☐ Month Day		

Log of Favorite Activities

DATE	ACTIVITY	COMMENTS
☐☐ / ☐☐ Month / Day		
☐☐ / ☐☐ Month / Day		
☐☐ / ☐☐ Month / Day		
☐☐ / ☐☐ Month / Day		
☐☐ / ☐☐ Month / Day		
☐☐ / ☐☐ Month / Day		
☐☐ / ☐☐ Month / Day		
☐☐ / ☐☐ Month / Day		

ACKNOWLEDGMENTS

Thanks to all the inspiring teachers at the preschool at Keneseth Israel in Elkins Park, Pennsylvania, who love our children and help them to learn through play: Merryl Bender (and Jen too!), Ethyl Treatman Burns, Fanny Chodosh, Melanie D'Orazio, Rhea Dennis, Myra (Schwartz) Greenberg, Jill Levine, Joanie Reinheimer, Liz Sussman, Micah Sussman, and Joan Zinberg, and thanks to Beth Berman for always making time to answer my questions. Special thanks for ideas and resources to Karen Chayot and Kathy Goldenberg (now of Project P.L.A.Y. School). Thanks to my editor, Jason Rekulak, for giving me the opportunity to write this book, and for all those encouraging e-mails that helped me along! And of course love and thanks to Cooper and Oren, my activity testers, and to Evan, my joke tester.

—L.R.

About the Authors:

LYNN ROSEN is also the author of *The Housewife Handbook*, a playful guide to life as a housewife, and *Table Matters*, a book about how to set the table and the history of our dining customs. She lives in the Philly suburbs with her husband and two young sons. Her six-year-old thinks she will turn twenty-four on her next birthday, but this is not true.

JOE BORGENICHT, D.A.D., is a writer, producer, and current toddler owner. He is the coauthor of *The Baby Owner's Manual*, *The Action Hero's Handbook*, *The Action Heroine's Handbook*, *Undercover Golf*, and *The Reality TV Handbook*.

About the Illustrators:

PAUL KEPPLE and JUDE BUFFUM are better known as the Philadelphia-based studio HEADCASE DESIGN. Their work has been featured in many design and illustration publications, such as *American Illustration*, *Communication Arts*, and *Print*. Paul worked at Running Press Publishers for several years before opening Headcase in 1998. Both graduated from the Tyler School of Art, where they now teach. Intern extraordinaire JESSICA HISCHE helped with many of the illustrations for this book.